THE NORTH CAUCASUS

The Central Asian and Caucasian Prospects project is sponsored by:

- A. Meredith Jones & Co. Ltd
- British Aerospace plc
- British American Tobacco
- BG plc
- BP Amoco plc
- ENI S.p.A.
- Mobil Oil Company Ltd
- Shell International Petroleum Company Ltd
- Statoil

Series editor: Edmund Herzig
Head, Russia and Eurasia Programme: Roy Allison

CENTRAL ASIAN AND CAUCASIAN PROSPECTS

THE NORTH CAUCASUS

Russia's Fragile Borderland

Anna Matveeva

THE ROYAL INSTITUTE OF
INTERNATIONAL AFFAIRS
Russia and Eurasia Programme

Published in Great Britain in 1999 by the Royal Institute of International Affairs,
Chatham House, 10 St James's Square, London SW1Y 4LE
(Charity Registration No. 208 223)

Distributed worldwide by The Brookings Institution, 1775 Massachusetts Avenue, NW,
Washington, DC 20036-2188, USA

ISBN 1 86203 062 6

Typeset in Times by Koinonia, Manchester
Printed and bound in Great Britain by the Chameleon Press Limited
Cover design by Youngs Design in Production

CONTENTS

ABOUT THE AUTHOR

Anna Matveeva is a Research Fellow in the Russia and Eurasia Programme at the Royal Institute of International Affairs. Since 1997 she has coordinated the Institute's Central Asian and Caucasian Prospects project. She was previously Head of the Former Soviet Union Programme at International Alert, a London-based NGO working towards conflict resolution. She has written a number of articles and book chapters on the region, including 'Democratization, Legitimacy and Political Change in Central Asia' (*International Affairs*, London, January 1999, vol. 75, no. 1).

ACKNOWLEDGMENTS

This paper was a genuinely socialist undertaking. Without the help of many people who so generously shared their time, information and ideas with me it would never have been accomplished. Jonathan Cohen was my first adviser on the region and his friendship and support always remained with me. I am heavily indebted to the people in the North Caucasus who introduced me to the politics and culture of their homelands, and also hosted me during my travels, in particular Enver Kisriev (Dagestan), Aleksandr Dzadziev (North Ossetia) and Svetlana Akkieva (Kabardino-Balkaria). I would also like to express my gratitude to Magomed-Salikh Gusayev and Eduard Urazayev (Dagestan), Lev Dzugayev (North Ossetia) and Nikolai Petrov (Moscow).

I am grateful to the participants of a study group, held at Chatham House to discuss a first draft of the paper, for their useful comments and suggestions, particularly Richard Sakwa, Michael Kaser, Fanny Missfeldt and Peter Duncan. My colleagues at Chatham House – Roy Allison and Edmund Herzig (Russia and Eurasia Programme) and Mary Bone (Library) – provided assistance throughout the project. Sarah Smith and Margaret May (Publications) transformed my imperfect words into accessible English. My very special thanks are to Clem McCartney who provided intellectual inspiration for me to write this paper.

The Ford Foundation-funded project at Chatham House, 'Keeping the Peace in the CIS', contributed towards the cost of this publication.

June 1999   A.M.

SUMMARY

The North Caucasus has emerged as the most volatile area of the Russian Federation since the break-up of the Soviet Union. It was an arena for the first inter-ethnic conflict in the new Russia, as well as witnessing the first war for political secession. The political situation of the 1990s enabled the republican elites to exploit the opportunities presented by the Soviet collapse. It also unleashed forces which were beyond the control of the authorities. Conflicting national projects, elite rivalry and new means to secure access to power created a situation of political disorder. Stability and development remain remote goals and security concerns continue to dominate the region's politics. Its borderland location, unique demographic and cultural composition, and political and economic trends make it the least integrated territory in the Russian Federation.

The study describes the North Caucasus as a region in flux and interprets the volatility of its developments as a struggle for political order both in the region and in the Russian Federation. It outlines its historical and demographic background, but argues that the challenges facing the region are essentially modern. It assesses the political, economic and social challenges to successful governance, and analyses the policy responses adopted by the regional elites. It also outlines the issues of change and instability which drive conflicts in the region, and considers their future prospects. The economic significance of the region is almost exclusively dependent on energy resource development and the viability of the infrastructure, as well as resort facilities, both currently jeopardized by political instability and rising crime. Finally, the study addresses Russian federal policy towards the region which went through the stages of the management of ethnic relations, attempts to regain control by force, budget federalism and the fight against crime.

The study concludes that Moscow is distancing itself from the region by default rather than by design. The region developed more into a liability than an asset for the centre. The strategic retreat from the Caucasus is motivated by fear of further unwelcome developments, most notably the spillover of crime and the Islamist challenge.

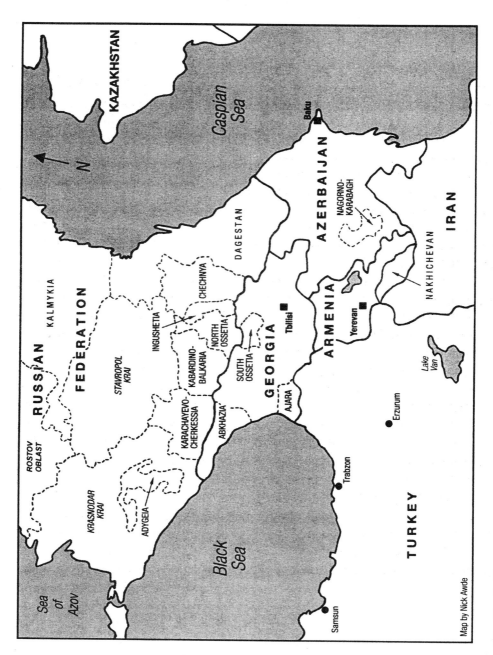

The North Caucasus

Map by Nick Awde

1 INTRODUCTION

The North Caucasus has emerged as the most volatile area of the Russian Federation since the break-up of the Soviet Union. Stability and development remain remote goals and security concerns dominate the region's politics. The current 'no war, no peace' situation in Chechnya presents a constant challenge to the Russian authorities, and the region's instability also affects its south Caucasian neighbours. The North Caucasus is sometimes referred to as 'Russia's inner abroad'. Its borderland location, unique demographic and cultural composition, and political and economic trends make it the least integrated territory in the Russian Federation.

Region in flux

The issues posed by the region are complex and numerous. This paper follows an interpretative framework based on a number of assumptions, the most important being the idea of political order. Political order is defined as the creation of effective authority and the accumulation of governing power.

First, there are issues of governance. In analysing political order in the North Caucasus the individual republics' internal developments, pressures, tensions and aspirations should be examined. By the late 1990s Russian federal policy had become increasingly redundant for the internal governance of the republics, which had become freer to make arrangements to build a political order of their own. They assumed more of the features of a state, pursuing territorial claims, and adopting laws to enable separation or cooperation with one another. In this sense they have to be defined as *de facto* self-governing entities, or as *proto-states*. Proto-states are not independent states in the sense of international recognition, but areas where the constraints exercised by the federal centre are felt less and less strongly. Meanwhile Moscow has largely withdrawn from direct interference in local affairs other than through budgetary allocations. This is a clear departure from the pattern of the Soviet state, when the centre carried out most of the functions of government.

At the same time, the degree of governance in such proto-states – in the sense of the ability of the system to innovate policy, implement laws and enforce order – is very low. The weakness of the state is primarily located on the republican level and is rooted in a lack of socio-political cohesion between government and society. These emergent proto-states 'possess neither a widely accepted and coherent idea of the state among their populations, nor a governing power strong enough to impose unity in the absence of political consensus'.[1] This phenomenon partly stems from the general weakness of political order in Russia. However, the distinct features of the North Caucasus make the challenges of governance even more formidable. The region is also home to a 'failed proto-state' (Chechnya) where the previous order has broken down beyond repair and the republic has disintegrated into a number of warring camps, a threat to itself and to its neighbours.

Second, there are issues regarding society. If the states are so weak, can the internal cohesion of their societies hold them together? On the one hand, the Soviet party-state did not supplant societal affiliations in the North Caucasus to the extent it did in most of the Russian Federation. Ethnic and religious identities and a sense of local culture and history remained strong. On the other hand, while ethnic identities became politicized, they failed to develop into national identities and create political communities. Instead, ethnic identities strengthened and sub-ethnic (regional, clan, extended family) affiliations became predominant. This contributed to the process of fragmentation rather than consolidation of the societies, and placed further obstacles in the way of any collective action. The resurgence of politicized Islam as an ideology capable of cutting across narrow ethnic loyalties may be one force which could overcome the existing fragmentation.

Third, there are issues related to the transition to democracy. What are the agents of change and in which direction do these changes point? With the collapse of communism it seemed that a transition to liberal democracy was imminent. Indeed, many of the formal institutions of democracy have been installed in the North Caucasus, as in the rest of the Russian Federation. Whether they hold real authority or serve merely as a means of legitimizing power which resides elsewhere is questionable, however. Two problems arise in connection with this. One is the issue of post-Soviet elites, formal and informal, and their relation to their Soviet counterparts. The other concerns the remnants of the old communist order, structures of autonomy and a perceived conflict between tradition and modernity. The crucial question, therefore, is where the locus of power lies and to what extent the formal elites and institutions are dominated by informal power networks.

Fourth, there are security issues. The argument of this paper is that the conflicts and potential conflicts in the region are a product of weak political order and the inability of local leaderships to find adequate responses to existing challenges. Thus the local leaderships become hostages to regional conflicts. Security considerations prevent the North Caucasus from addressing more substantive issues of governance

---

[1] Barry Buzan, *People, States and Fear: An Agenda for International Security Studies in the Post-Cold War Era* (London: Harvester Wheatsheaf, 1991), p. 101.

and economic development. And they reduce government to a balancing act between different ethnic and social groups which is aimed at reducing the possibility of violence in the short term.

The main threats to security come from within the region rather than from outside, and the enhancement of security can only come from within. Meanwhile, the problems of political order in the North Caucasus and the deteriorating security environment produce implications for the neighbouring southern Russian regions of Krasnodar, Stavropol and Rostov, and for the South Caucasus.

Finally, there are issues related to the role of the federal centre. Are we dealing with a colonial relationship or with minority issues in a multi-ethnic state? The Chechens were the only group with a coherent secessionist agenda, but this only became a predominant aspiration as a result of the federal military intervention. The arguments against defining the North Caucasus as a Russian colony include the fact that the peoples of these republics are full citizens of the Federation, they are ruled by indigenous elites and the federal budgetary allocations from the centre are clearly in their favour. Moreover, in policy terms Moscow tries to adapt itself to the specifics of its constituent parts. Such a reconfiguration of centre–periphery relations in Russia is described by Richard Sakwa as republicanization – a phenomenon combining both federalism and confederalism, but with a complex relational approach instead of clear devolution of political authority to sub-national governments.[2]

Coping with the political and social processes unleashed by the collapse of the USSR is beyond the present ability of the Russian establishment, and the North Caucasus poses its hardest challenge. The political process under way in the region is not a coherent drive for secession or a struggle for independence, but a creeping disengagement by default. In the long term the North Caucasus may come to be seen more as a liability than as an asset for Moscow. It may be argued that the costs of keeping the North Caucasus within the Russian Federation are too high and that Russian geo-economic and security interests may be better served by other means.

Regional identity

The identity of the North Caucasus stems from the fact that it is subject to a common set of factors, rather than the similarity of its peoples or the evincing of any desire to integrate into a single North Caucasian nation. A number of forces acquired a space to operate as a result of the Soviet collapse and subsequent power vacuum in all the republics. These include the drive for secession, politicized ethnicity and Islam, social fragmentation and the predominance of informal power arrangements. But the

[2] Richard Sakwa, 'The Republicanisation of Russia: Sovereignty, Federalism, and Democratic Order', unpublished paper delivered to the Political Science Association conference at the University of Nottingham, March 1999.

policy responses, adopted by the ruling elites as well as by the Russian leadership, have been different in each case. As a result, political and social developments in the post-Soviet period differ in each republic.

The region possesses a common geography and a common history. Its ethnic and religious diversity, history of anti-imperial struggle and current social and demographic trends remain central for current political processes. The legacy of territorial and ethnic partitions, arbitrary borders and the combination of unrelated peoples in ethno-territorial units continues to dominate the modern politics of the region and give grounds for mutually exclusive interpretations of history.

Ethnic and religious diversity

The ethnic republics of the North Caucasus – Adygeia, Karachaevo-Cherkessia, Kabardino-Balkaria, North Ossetia, Ingushetia, Chechnya and Dagestan – occupy the southernmost territory of the Russian Federation and lie between two seas – the Black Sea and the Caspian – both of which have strategic significance. It is one of the most ethnically diverse areas in the world and its high mountains have precluded different groups from intermixing and contributed to the survival of diverse linguistic and cultural identities. The region was historically populated by various Caucasian, Turkic or Iranian peoples, and today about 40 groups living in the North Caucasus are believed still to have a distinct ethnic identity.[3] The Soviet pattern of nationality registration was linguistically defined, and language affinity was held to establish the degree of distance between peoples. Many of the languages of the Caucasus belong to a distinct Caucasian language group and speakers of Caucasian languages constitute the majority of the titular nationalities in the North Caucasian republics. These are subdivided into western and eastern groups. The west Caucasian group comprises the Circassians (Cherkess) including the Adyge and Kabard peoples; and the east Caucasian group is represented by the related Chechens and Ingush, collectively known as Vainakh, as well as by the Avars, Dargins, Laks and Lezgins. A second group of peoples speaking the Turkic language includes Kumyks, Karachai, Balkar, Nogai and Azeri peoples. A third group speaking Iranian languages is represented by Ossetes and Tats.

An inter-confessional mix of Christian and Muslim groups adds to the region's diversity. Slavs and Ossetes are Christian Orthodox, while other nationalities are traditionally Muslim[4] and the Tats are mostly Jews.

---

[3] Helen Krag and Lars Funch, *The North Caucasus: Minorities at a Crossroads*, Minority Rights Group Report, 1994–5, p. 16.

[4] Approximately 14 million people in the Russian Federation belong to Muslim ethnic groups. No data are available on how many of them are practising believers.

History under Tsarist rule

The first wave of Russian expansion towards the North Caucasus came in 1556, after the annexation of Astrakhan, and ended with a military disaster in 1604 when the Muscovite army was crushed by the peoples of Dagestan supported by the Ottomans. Russia only resumed its interest in the North Caucasus in 1783 with a slow but systematic advance. Parts of Dagestan, the Ingush and Chechen territories were conquered, provoking the first attempt at organized insurgence led by Sheikh Mansur, a Chechen. Local resistance was strong but social and linguistic differences severely hampered the people's ability to oppose Russian troops. Their disunity was overcome during the *ghazawat* (holy war) of 1824–95, when unification along religious lines was initiated by the Dagestani Imam Qazi Mohammed, and then Imam Shamil, both ethnic Avars. The Imamate, a state formation created on the basis of *sharia* law, mobilized a systematic resistance to the Russian advance and inflicted heavy losses on the Russian side. The Circassians offered the most ferocious resistance to the Russian advances and were decimated as a result. Only the fall of Circassia in 1864, five years after the capitulation of Imam Shamil in Dagestan, marked the end of the Caucasian war.

The significance of the North Caucasus for Russia was almost exclusively based on its geographic position as an obstacle to Russia's access to the South Caucasus. For the Caucasian groups, however, Russian conquest led to a large exodus of indigenous peoples, mainly Circassians but also Chechens and Dagestanis, to the Ottoman Empire. Their descendants today form a diaspora of up to 2 million people in Turkey and the Middle East.

The Soviet period

After the 1917 October Revolution the North Caucasian leaders agreed to recognize Soviet power and form an Autonomous Soviet Mountain Republic in 1921 in return for the expulsion of the Cossacks (seen by the Soviets as a major enemy of the new regime), and the promise to leave *sharia* laws as the legal foundation for the new republic. While the Soviet power kept its promise to deport the Cossacks (over 70,000 were deported east of the Urals), an offensive against Islam was launched in the 1920s and provoked another wave of ferocious resistance. The Mountain Republic proved to be short-lived owing to the tensions between its constituents, and the process of giving politicized form to ethno-territorial fragmentation started. By the mid-1920s a hierarchy of ethnically defined autonomies was established with four Autonomous Republics (ASSRs): Kabardino-Balkaria, amalgamating two ethnically unrelated peoples in a single unit; North Ossetia; Checheno-Ingushetia, uniting two close groups; and Dagestan. Adygeia became an autonomous *okrug* (district) within Krasnodar *krai* and Karachaevo-Cherkessia became an autonomous *oblast* (province) within Stavropol *krai*. The Circassians were split into three smaller nationalities: the Adyge, Kabardins and Cherkess. The Circassians are closely related to the Abkhaz and Abaza, a kinship which played a significant role in the mobilization of west Caucasians to fight in Abkhazia's secessionist dispute with Georgia in 1992–3.

The next landmark in the turbulent history of the North Caucasus was the deportations during the Second World War, when the Karachai, Balkars, Chechens and Ingush were accused of collaboration with the German army and deported to Central Asia and Siberia.[5] The former republics of the deported peoples were dissolved (Checheno-Ingushetia ceased to exist between 1944 and 1958 and its territories were redistributed among its neighbours). Other Caucasian ethnic groups, mainly from the high mountains, were forcibly resettled in the lowland rural areas and had to adopt new agricultural practices, while Russians were drawn in to populate the urban settlements. In the late 1950s the deported peoples were allowed to return and were subsequently rehabilitated. Clashes took place between the returnees and those who had been resettled in their former homes, with each side claiming the right to the territory. The last major border revision took place in 1957–8 when several Russian (formerly Cossack) agricultural *raions* (districts) were transferred to the North Caucasian ethnic republics. Thus, North Ossetia gained Mozdok *raion*, Kabardino-Balkaria gained Prokhladnenskii and Maiskii *raions*, Checheno-Ingushetia gained Naurskii, Schelkovskii and Nadterechnyi *raions*, and Dagestan gained Tarumovskii and Kyzlyar *raion*.

The relaxation of Soviet authority during perestroika opened up the old wounds inflicted by deportations and partitions in the North Caucasus. While creating an opportunity for these grievances to be exposed, however, it failed to provide a mechanism to address the problems. The Law on the Rehabilitation of Repressed Peoples, passed in April 1991 by the USSR Supreme Soviet, sought to restore historical justice for those who were deported in the 1940s, but it was more a declaration of intent than a clear policy statement. It raised exaggerated hopes among the affected peoples that the territorial disputes would ultimately be resolved in their favour and added to existing ethnic tensions.

The post-Soviet period

In contrast to the rest of the Russian Federation, which has largely managed to avoid violence since 1991, the North Caucasus has been the scene of two wars and a number of armed clashes and has also been affected by conflicts across the border in the South Caucasus. Three main stages in post-Soviet history can be identified. The

---

[5] Most were resettled in Kazakhstan, while the local party elite, who assisted in organizing the deportation of their own peoples, were sent to Kyrgyzstan to avoid reprisals.

first lasted from the end of 1991 to December 1994 and the beginning of the war in Chechnya. The most significant development of this period was the elevation of these ethnic-based administrative units to the status of 'sovereign' republics within the Russian Federation. The Federation Treaty, signed in March 1992 by all the subjects of the Russian Federation except Chechnya and Tatarstan,[6] laid the foundation of the unequal power distribution between the centre and different administrative units. This was also the time of the rise and fall of the Confederation of the Peoples of the Caucasus (KNK). Founded in 1989, the KNK gained prominence with its involvement in the war in Abkhazia in 1992–3, but lost its ideological and organizational coherence as a result of paralysing internal feuds.[7]

The second stage (December 1994 to September 1996) was dominated by the war in Chechnya. The military intervention in Chechnya by Russian federal troops did not inspire separatist aspirations among the other North Caucasian republics, nor did it instigate a general Caucasian war. However, spillover fighting, the militarization of the area and refugee flows caused significant problems for Chechnya's neighbours. Moreover, as a result of the war a sense of the weakening of Russia took root among the North Caucasians.

The third and current stage is marked by the aftermath of the war in Chechnya and by pipeline politics. Current oil resource developments in Azerbaijan and Central Asia increase the geo-economic significance of the North Caucasus as an energy transportation corridor to the West. The choice of the route for the main export pipeline for Azerbaijani oil will, among other things, depend on the viability of the route through the North Caucasus. At the same time, local political actors may use the pipeline as a bargaining chip in their struggles with Moscow, or with one another. For the region itself, the internal turmoil in Chechnya is no less destabilizing than the straightforward conflict between Chechnya and Russian federal power.

The social and demographic situation

The population of the North Caucasus is predominantly rural, with the exception of North Ossetia where 70 per cent of the population live in towns. Chechnya, Ingushetia, Dagestan and Karachaevo-Cherkessia have the highest rural population in the Russian Federation. The North Caucasus also has the highest population density and birth rate in the Federation. Population pressure was exacerbated by the influx of refugees from the conflict in South Ossetia moving into North Ossetia, by displaced

---

[6] Ingushetia signed at a later stage.

[7] Fiona Hill, *Russia's Tinderbox: Conflict in the North Caucasus and its Implications for the Future of the Russian Federation*, Strengthening Democratic Institutions Project, Harvard University, JFK School of Government, September 1995, pp. 24–9.

persons (DPs)[8] from North Ossetia entering Ingushetia and DPs from Chechnya moving to Ingushetia, Dagestan and Stavropol *krai*.

Demographic pressures, coupled with economic factors (see Chapter 4), present a serious challenge to the maintenance of social stability in the region and have had an adverse effect on southern Russia. It is an area of widespread unemployment, with up to 30 per cent of the labour force working outside the republic in the Soviet period, forming seasonal brigades, or engaging in small trade operations or in labour-intensive jobs. The rise of anti-Caucasian sentiment in Central Asia (there were pogroms in Noviy Uzen, Kazakhstan, in June 1989 and in the Fergana Valley) led to the expulsion of the Caucasians. The dissolution of the USSR, combined with economic decline in the Russian Federation and the fostering of anti-Caucasian prejudice, dramatically reduced opportunities for work and forced people to return home. Economic decline was aggravated by the collapse of defence enterprises which had once absorbed excess labour.

The region is also witnessing the rapid exodus of ethnic Russians. For the Russian federal government the North Caucasus is Russia's southern flank, its newly established border with Georgia and Azerbaijan and a frontline military district with a high concentration of troops. It is significant as a potential route for the oil pipelines from the Caspian Sea to the markets in Europe.

The most important influence on the region is its immediate neighbourhood. It shares a border with Georgia and Azerbaijan, mostly separated by high mountains. The neighbours to the north, Krasnodar and Stavropol *krais* of the Russian Federation, present a contrasting picture to the North Caucasus. Both *krais* possess some of the best agricultural land in Russia, as well as reasonably functioning industry, while Krasnodar *krai*, the third most populous within the Federation, enjoys access to the Azov and Black Seas and the remaining Russian resorts. These rich and conservative *krais* used to be a breeding ground for the Soviet elites, and continue to play an important role in federal politics. The *krais* present a communist stronghold, the 'red belt' of the Federation ruled by communists who won decisive victories against Moscow's nominees. Russians and Ukrainians constitute an overwhelming majority (88.5 per cent in Krasnodar and 86.6 per cent in Stavropol *krai*) while other minorities, mostly of Caucasian origin and many of them recent migrants, are treated with suspicion and growing reluctance to accept new arrivals. Both *krais* have developed severe anti-migration laws and are renowned for their ethnic prejudices. In a way, these regions serve as a buffer between the volatile North Caucasus and the

---

[8] In UN terminology refugees are those who cross an international border; those who are forced to move within one country are termed internally displaced persons, or IDPs. The terms are normally the subject of ferocious disagreement between the conflicting parties. The term displaced persons, or DPs, is adopted in this paper.

inner parts of Russia. As the largest recipients of DPs and subject to terrorist attacks, they are increasingly assuming the features of a borderland.

Russian federal policy, albeit less determined to control internal developments, is important for centre–periphery relations. Non-CIS actors have so far played a marginal role. International organizations, such as the OSCE, ICRC and UNHCR, have been involved in humanitarian relief and conflict resolution in Chechnya. The North Caucasian diaspora in Turkey and in the Middle East have campaigned to put the situation in the republic on the agenda of their governments and have rendered modest financial assistance, while some Arab countries have attempted to use regional instability to promote Islamic propaganda. However, although local perceptions of outside involvement are high, the activities of external powers have been severely constrained by the desire to preserve good relations with Moscow.

Key issues

While stressing the significance of the region's history and political culture, it is worth remembering that past history does not necessarily determine present-day developments. The challenges the region is facing are modern ones and stem from unprecedented political change. This paper will focus on three themes:

- Identifying the forces which operate in the region, constituting challenges to successful governance and confronting republican and federal authorities.
- Assessing the policy responses chosen by various actors on republican and federal levels to address these challenges and to pursue their political goals.
- Considering the security implications of the regional conflicts and tensions, of the rise of politicized Islam and of the impact of security challenges beyond the North Caucasus. The effects of instability in the region for the territorial integrity of the Russian Federation are also discussed.

The interaction between the troubled past and the turbulent present to create arrangements for the future is currently under way in the North Caucasus. The meaning of this dramatic, often violent process is the struggle for political order.

2 POLITICAL ORDER

Degree of governance

A common feature of the North Caucasian republics is that all of them suffer to a varying degree from difficulty in instituting effective, legitimate government. They are characterized by increasing ethnic, social and religious conflicts, by the dominance of personalities, by corruption among ministers and civil servants, by declining standards of bureaucratic efficiency, by the weak authority of legislatures and courts and the lack of impact of party politics on the political process. In short, the basic problem is not the form but the degree of governance in the sense of the ability of the political system to innovate policy, implement laws and enforce order.[1]

The decay of governance is apparent in a number of ways:

- *Control over coercive forces.* The Soviet break-up sparked a spontaneous militarization of the area. The creation of informal armed structures in 1991–2 was encouraged by some North Caucasian leaders, such as Djohar Dudayev in Chechnya and Akhsarbek Galazov in North Ossetia. It also developed out of various ethnic movements and fronts, as in Dagestan. The leaders of the military formations developed political and 'business' agendas of their own, and attempts to integrate them into national armies, currently being undertaken in Chechnya, and into local self-defence units in Dagestan, have had only limited success.
- *The ability to pursue comprehensive undertakings.* The social and economic problems of the region are vast, yet no strategies or coherent programmes on how to promote social and economic reform have been developed. Moreover, federal legislation, such as land reform, and long-term policy undertakings, such as the *Gory* (Survival in the Mountains) and Coastal Protection programmes have never been implemented.
- *The collapse of the public sphere.* No one seems to be responsible for facilities such as public housing, health care, transport, education and social security. The withering of civil authority is reflected in the absence of urban planning, poor

---

[1] The analytical approach of this chapter derives from Samuel Huntington, *Political Order in Changing Societies* (New Haven and London: Yale University Press, 1968).

10

maintenance of public buildings and declining standards of public health.[2]

- *Implementation and enforcement.* Although it might be argued that the federal laws are not always applicable to local circumstances, the implementation even of local legislation is ineffective.

Ethnicity and political community

The Soviet nationality policies fostered the emergence of national identities out of narrow communal loyalties and consolidated ethnic consciousness. They institution-alized the link between identities and ethnically defined territories; created written languages based on the Cyrillic alphabet; imposed Cyrillic on Arabic script languages; and promoted officially sponsored cultural and educational institutions. The Soviet system recognized the power of ethnicity and used it to relieve pressures in society, but the expression of nationalist sentiment and political demands based on ethnicity was suppressed.

In the late 1980s perestroika brought about the phenomenon of politicized ethnicity and unleashed ethnic grievances. These were directed against the rule of Moscow, as in the case of Chechnya, or towards the restoration of historical justice, as with the Ingush and Balkars, or towards upgrading a people's standing *vis-à-vis* other ethnic groups, as in Dagestan. In more general terms, all of these grievances centred on the drive to protect ethnic groups as distinct communities. This drive was impelled both by uncertainty over their place within the new Russian-dominated state form-ation – the Russian Federation – and also, even more, by unresolved territorial claims, competition over resources and fears of cultural vulnerability.[3]

The mass mobilization of 1991–3 along ethnic lines resulted in the emergence of various national movements or fronts. Every ethnic group formed an organization of its own, and the most prominent, such as the Chechen National Congress and Ingush Ni'skho (Justice) turned into radical political movements, though many others, such as Tenglik (Kumyk), Shamil Popular Front (Avar), Sadesh (Dargin), Sadval (Lezgin), Tsubars (Lak) and Birlik (Nogai), and the Kabardin and Balkar National Congresses formed during the late 1980s, had already passed their peak by the mid-1990s. They fulfilled a dual function: to put ethnic groups' claims on the governmental agenda, and to serve as a platform for emerging leaders.

---

[2] For example, the number of cases of infectious diseases in Dagestan is 2.2 times higher than the Russian average, according to *Sotsial'noye polozheniye Respubliki Dagestan*, published by the State Statistical Committee of the Republic of Dagestan, Makhachkala, 1997.

[3] See Jane Ormrod, 'The North Caucasus: Confederation in Conflict', in Ian Bremmer and Ray Taras, eds, *New States, New Politics: Building the Post-Soviet Nations* (Cambridge: Cambridge University Press, 1997), pp. 96–139.

The power of ethnicity was emphasized by the increased importance of traditional affiliations, such as ethnic, *teip* (Chechen clan) and regional groupings. Ethnic, clan and kinship associations expanded into the vacuum left by the collapse of the civic affiliations of the Soviet period, such as education, social background and occupation, and provided something for people to fall back on in the conditions of uncertainty. Resentment over the new Russian passport design, which does not mention ethnic affiliation, again emphasized the depth of ethnic feelings, although such feelings are regarded by Russian federal authorities as an inherited communist prejudice not worth carrying into the liberal-democratic future.[4] The collapse of Soviet (civic) identity, and the absence of overarching national identities on the basis of which internal coherence could have emerged, strengthened the divisions in societies. This stress on ethnic division precludes the formation of a political community involving moral consensus and mutual interest, which would unite different groups on the grounds that all of them would have a certain stake in the political regime.

Conflicting national projects

Since the 1980s the republics of the North Caucasus have made rapid progress from societies with relatively uniform and straightforward structures of authority and a small number of actors in politics, to extremely diverse societies with a multiplicity of groups competing for power, influence and control over resources. The collapse of the communist regime in 1991 created new opportunities in politics when the old set of rules was no longer applicable, but the new one had yet to emerge. President Yeltsin's invitation 'to take as much sovereignty as you can swallow', the Law on Rehabilitation of Deported Peoples in 1991, the withdrawal of Russian federal forces from Chechnya in 1991 and the implicit understanding that Moscow would not try to impose order by force provided impetus for those active in politics. The elites in the North Caucasus were more ready to grasp the new opportunities because of the presence of ethnic channels for mobilization and the existence of state structures in the old institutions of the autonomous republics.

Various actors embarked on projects of political modernization and sought to define visions of a better future for their respective constituencies. Their modernization projects envisaged a commitment to representative democracy, the rationalization of authority and increased popular participation. These ideas filled the declarations of the republican authorities and national movements of the early 1990s, though in the end they often resulted in the promotion of exclusively ethnic causes. The essence of the project led by the Chechen National Congress was national liberation from an

---

[4] *Bulletin of the Network on Ethnological Monitoring and Early Warning of Conflicts*, Institute of Ethnology and Anthropology (Russian Academy of Sciences, Moscow) and Conflict Management Group (Harvard), 4: 15, December 1997, pp. 7–24 (in Russian).

imperial Russia. Although differences existed over the price and means of securing sovereignty in Chechnya, a broad consensus over the ultimate goal of national independence enabled the Chechen National Congress and General Dudayev to stay in power despite the regime's disastrous economic and social policies. In North Ossetia, as well as among the Lezgins of Dagestan, the core of the national projects was unification: with ethnic kin across the border in South Ossetia (Georgia) and with the Lezgin minority in Azerbaijan. For the Ingush in Checheno-Ingushetia and the Balkar in Kabardino-Balkaria the projects were aimed at separation from the double-nationality entity (which the Ingush achieved in 1992 and the Balkar National Congress failed to do) and the restoration of historical justice in regaining lands lost during the deportation period. The remaining titular nationalities – the Karachai and Kabardin – retaliated with attempts to secure their territories from outsiders' claims. In Dagestan the competition between lowland groups (Kumyk, Nogai, Azeri and Russian) versus the invasion of the highlanders (Avars, Dargins, Lezgins, Agul, Rutul and Tabasarans) led to lowland projects aimed at securing 'ethnic homelands' to establish access to lands lost to the highlanders as a result of the resettlement practices of Soviet times. The federalization of Dagestan became a lowlanders' project.[5]

The groups opting for change were initially committed to the use of political means in implementing their self-determination projects through declarations, elections of national leaders and mutual agreements. The independence acquired by the Union Republics of Georgia, Armenia and Azerbaijan provided inspiration for the Chechens in 1991. However, when the euphoria of perestroika passed, it became apparent in 1992–3 that the national projects were in conflict with one another, as the realization of one group's national cause entailed infringement of another group's position. The complex ethnic composition of the North Caucasus precluded the creation of new ethno-territorial boundaries on the basis of consensus.

Elite mobilization

The Soviet-era elite in the North Caucasus, as elsewhere in the Soviet Union, was raised through the system of *nomenklatura*, when elites were recreated according to an all-Union pattern and local leaders, prior to their promotion to the most senior positions, were normally rotated through the centrally administered system. Moscow held the key to crucial appointments.

During perestroika local intellectuals, mainly in the human rights field, articulated national grievances and helped to shape the language of political discourse. Unlike their counterparts in the South Caucasus, however, they failed to gain political office and lost most of their influence. Since 1991, ethnic networks have served as channels

---

[5] Laks, although highlanders, joined the federalization aspiration. See Ali Aliev, '*Kakim zhe byt' Dagestanu - unitarnym ili federativnym?*' (Makhachkala, 1997).

for the creation of new elites or for the building of public support for any representatives of the old system capable of promoting the national cause. The multiplicity of ethnic and kinship networks has encouraged a range of actors in politics. In contrast to the rest of the Russian Federation an acute, often violent, power struggle between candidates for various offices is evident in the North Caucasus.

The present elites broadly fall into three categories: former Party *nomenklatura* (see Box 1), Soviet ex-servicemen and the leaders of ethnic networks.

Box 1: Republics headed by former party leaders

Adygeia – *Aslan Dzhabrailov*, the former Krasnodar Communist Party *kraikom* secretary for agriculture, has ruled the republic since 1989, first as the *obkom* first secretary, then as Chairman of the Supreme Soviet. He was elected president in 1992 and re-elected in January 1997.

Karachaevo-Cherkessia – *Vladimir Khubiev*, the former *obkom* Communist Party secretary, headed the republic since 1979, first as a Chairman of the Executive Committee of the *oblast* Council (1979–91), then as a Head of the Administration (1992–3), Prime Minister (1994–5), and Head of the Republic (1995–9). He lost the elections in April 1999.

Kabardino-Balkaria – *Valerii Kokov*, the former first secretary of the local *obkom*, then the Chairman of the Supreme Soviet, has headed the republic since 1990. He was elected president in 1992 and re-elected in 1997.

North Ossetia – former president *Akhsarbek Galazov*, previously republican first party secretary, headed the republic from 1990. Having been Chairman of the Supreme Soviet he was elected president in 1994. In 1998 he lost to Aleksandr Dzasokhov, former North Ossetian *obkom* first secretary (1988–90), who was promoted to the Central Committee and then to Politburo membership.

Dagestan – *Magomedali Magomedov*, Chairman of the State Council of Dagestan (since 1994), former Chairman of the Council of Ministers of the Republic (1983–7); he was also Chairman of the Supreme Soviet of Dagestan (1987–94).

The crucial factor in enhancing the role of the *nomenklatura* representatives was the presence of the Soviet structures of political autonomy in the North Caucasian ethnic republics. These 'empty shells' of autonomous structures enabled most of the old guard to rename Supreme Soviets as National Assemblies and party headquarters as presidential apparatuses, change the communist cause into a national one and continue as usual. The presence of ex-communists in office does not mean that they pursue a communist agenda; on the contrary, many abandoned their former convictions and became bitter opponents of communism.[6] They claimed administrative or

[6] Akhsarbek Galazov, who openly maintained a communist stance, was an exception.

managerial experience as their principal asset, and stressed their good relations with Moscow, which enabled them to obtain federal subsidies. Meanwhile, the significance of the economic *nomenklatura* has vastly diminished because of the demise of the all-Union, predominantly defence, enterprises in the region.

The ex-Soviet generals emerged on the political scene in 1990–91 and were regarded as men of action and national heroes around whom ethnic groups could unite. The generals formed the counter-elites that headed the national movements.[7] The airforce general Djohar Dudayev was elected president of Chechnya in 1991 and proclaimed independence from the Russian Federation. General Ruslan Aushev, the commander of a Motor Rifle Division in the Far Eastern Military District, became the leader of Ingushetia in 1992 and headed the establishment of the new republic. General Sufian Beppayev, the former deputy commander of the Transcaucasus military district and the Chairman of the Balkar National Congress, declared sovereignty in 1996; General Muguddin Kahrimanov, the leader of Sadval, the Lezgin national movement, called for unification of the two divided Lezgin groups into one sovereign formation, and thus failed to win public office; nevertheless both were subsequently coopted into government. Aslan Maskhadov, current president of Chechnya and an ex-colonel of the Russian army,[8] was a representative of a dominant group which enabled him to gain political office.

The third group consists of powerful individuals from the younger generation, in their thirties and forties, who started their careers in the post-Soviet era and managed to make their way up through personal forcefulness and the skilful exploitation of economic and social anarchy. Their prominence is especially significant in Chechnya and Dagestan. Many of them, like Gaji Makhachev, the Chairman of DagNeft in Dagestan, or Khozh-Ahmed Nukhayev, the Chairman of the Caucasus Common Market and former deputy prime minister of Chechnya, have criminal convictions, some of them for violent crimes. Often from underprivileged backgrounds and with strong ties to rural areas, many started off as bodyguards to the leading figures in the republics in the late 1980s, such as the ethnic Lak Magomed Khachilayev, USSR ex-champion in karate and later head of Dagestani fisheries, and the late Ruslan Labazanov, former head of the presidential bodyguard in Chechnya.[9] Some of them,

---

[7] A military career was one of the few routes to advancement for North Caucasians in Soviet times.

[8] Maskhadov finished his military career as a Chief of Staff of the missile and artillery garrison and the Deputy Commander of the division.

[9] Sports schools, designed for the leisure activities for Soviet youth, bred many of the present strongmen. Wrestling and similar sports are traditionally popular in the North Caucasus and produced a number of world champions who represented the USSR, and gave them new prominence. It became fashionable for the new leaders to open and finance sports schools for boys bearing their family names (Magomed Khachilayev, for instance, opened a sports school named after his brother Adam, who was killed in the dispute with the Chechens). His younger brother, Nadirshakh, the leader of Union of Muslims and an ex-State Duma deputy, is also a distinguished karate wrestler.

like Nukhayev, came to prominence through business activities in Moscow, and returned to their native land with money and power. Their career paths include the acquisition of sources of illegal, often dangerous, income, then election into local or republican bodies or gaining official control over the republic's most lucrative assets.

These powerful individuals, often businessmen and leaders of ethnic movements, rely on their ethnic, clan and regional kinship networks[10] among which they command loyalty and for which they can negotiate. They are surrounded by groups of bodyguards or private armies. In Chechnya this process of career enhancement was accelerated during the war when powerful field commanders emerged. Because the war was largely self-financed, only those independent commanders who found ways to secure funds managed to come to prominence. The new power groupings can make gestures towards representatives of their own communities, especially in the wake of the elections, and many want to be regarded as local Robin Hoods. However, they are unlikely to care about the general public good or work towards state interests.

As a result of these developments, politics became localized. The reliance on ethnic or clan groups and their support systems makes the elites hostage to ethnic/ regional competition and prevents the emergence of more inclusive politics. Political actors are locally bred and locally minded, and the ability of the federal authorities to influence internal political developments has considerably diminished. The political class is not inclined to develop a civic sense or to accept responsibility for the wider community and does not seem to have much stake in the development of sustainable governance. The present system of elite functioning, which has an ethnic basis, is a clear departure from the Soviet pattern which, while taking ethnic balance into consideration, at least publicly promoted a civic principle based on meritocracy.

Development of political institutions

The republics of the North Caucasus, while being subjects of the Russian Federation, are free to make whatever political provisions they wish. Despite significant disparities in the arrangements they have made, all maintain unitarism and function as *de facto* presidential republics.

All the North Caucasian republics adopted their own constitutions between 1994 and 1997 and made political arrangements which aspire to reflect local circumstances. Many of the constitutions contain special privileges for indigenous ethnic groups and refer to ethnic groups as state-bearing components. Some argue that

[10] Enver Kisriev calls them ethno-parties; see 'The Pressure of the Ethnic Question', *WarReport*, 58, February–March 1998, p. 83.

16

this reflects the tendency to make ethnic groups legally recognized political actors.[11] The constitutional arrangements are frequently a reflection of aspirations rather than a guide to actual politics, however. Those who drafted them were often more concerned to achieve ethnic equality and express their commitment to the goals and values of inter-ethnic peace or, in Chechnya, their commitment to Islamic tradition than to explain how these provisions should be implemented and enforced. The political provisions try to address what are considered the most serious problems for the republican leaderships. In Dagestan and in Kabardino-Balkaria, for instance, the most acute danger is a violation of inter-ethnic stability; in Chechnya law and order is the main issue. Most of the republics formed extra-constitutional security councils, modelled on the Russian federal example, but with varying political status.

Constitutions, presidents and legislature

Although affected by the same set of factors, the republics demonstrate marked differences in political developments. North Ossetia, for instance, can be regarded as a notable exception in the region. The power here remained within formal political institutions, and when Aleksandr Dzasokhov won the presidential elections with 76 per cent of the vote in January 1998 it was the only successful example of political change through the ballot box. At the same time, turbulent relations with their regional neighbours distract much of the authorities' attention from the strengthening of government.

In tiny Ingushetia power is concentrated in the hands of the president, Ruslan Aushev. His role in building the republic and efforts towards the resolution of the conflict with North Ossetia were pivotal. This enabled him to be seen as a national leader in the virtually mono-ethnic republic and easily rally institutional support for his political undertakings. Parliament is not permitted to intervene in politics, and the president has threatened to disband it if its members step out of line.

Chechnya is an example of a constitutional legislation which reflects general aspirations but is hard to implement in political practice. It combines a commitment to *sharia* law with an attempt to incorporate both *adat*, the customary law embedded in local traditional norms of behaviour, and secular democratic provisions in developing political institutions. The country's political arrangements were aimed at preventing a concentration of power, in reaction to Dudayev's dictatorial tendencies, and were designed to allow the inclusion of the different interests and groups which advanced during the war.

[11] Larissa Khoperskaia, 'Ideya etnicheskoi pravosubeknosti na Severnom Kavkaze', in J. Azrael, E. Pain, N. Zubarevitch, eds, *Evolyutsiya vzaimootnoshenii tsentra i regionov Rossii: ot konfliktov k poisku soglasiya* (Moscow: Center for Ethno-Political and Regional Studies & RAND Center for Russian and Eurasian Studies, 1997), p. 219.

In Dagestan inter-ethnic relations are constantly at risk and the government is understandably apprehensive about any violation of inter-ethnic peace. This issue has a high political profile, and as a result the Dagestani Ministry for Nationalities is more powerful than its federal counterpart. Faced with the choice between making Dagestan a federation or maintaining a unitary state, the government opted for the latter, arguing that there was no obvious way to split the republic into units and fearing that the process of federalization would encourage mutually exclusive claims by different ethnic groups.

Elections

Among the attributes of democracy, competitive elections are easily identifiable and most recognized. As Bruce Parrott argues, they are a precondition for the other political benefits that a democratic system may confer on its citizens.[12] In this respect the North Caucasian republics have made some progress, although significant gaps still remain. The republican former *nomenklatura* presidents were usually opposed by former dissident rivals in their elections for the first term and by communist candidates in the second; in both cases they were normally won by a wide margin.

The major difficulty in conducting elections in the North Caucasus is that the electorate votes according to ethnic/clan affiliations. This means that the results are determined by demographic balance, and that cross-national parties and programmes have difficulty establishing themselves. Elections in such circumstances tend to produce a divisive effect rather than ensuring government accountability.

As a result of these conditions systems have been developed to encourage cross-ethnic voting. In Dagestan the electoral system is designed to ensure that the balance between the ethnic groups in the People's Assembly mirrors that in the population. According to the electoral law, 65 constituencies are classified as multi-ethnic and were allocated to candidates from only one ethnic group living in the constituency. Only members of that ethnic group (not necessarily living in the constituency) could compete against one another, but all the registered electorate, irrespective of ethnicity, vote in the constituency. The government determined which ethnic group would be allocated which constituency and an arrangement that was broadly accepted as fair was worked out. Constituencies regarded as mono-ethnic had an ordinary open-candidate system. It might be argued that the present system, by formally fixing the divisions, increases social fragmentation and that a multi-seat system of proportional representation would be more appropriate. In Kabardino-Balkaria and

[12] Bruce Parrott, 'Perspectives on Postcommunist Democratization', in Karen Dawisha and Bruce Parrott, eds, *Conflict, Cleavage, and Change in Central Asia and the Caucasus* (Cambridge: Cambridge University Press, 1997), p. 4.

Adygeia privileges for indigenous minority groups are expressed in the way constituencies are defined. In the former the upper chamber of the parliament also serves the purpose of ethnic representation.

The fear of violating inter-ethnic peace in Karachaevo-Cherkessia was such that it led the republic to abstain from ever holding elections for the position of head of the executive, making it unique in the Russian Federation. For 19 years it was ruled by Vladimir Khubiev, until in 1998 a crisis unfolded around the electoral issue and under pressure from the opposition elections finally took place in April-May 1999.[13] These triggered acute political rivalry which resulted in a number of terrorist acts and sporadic outbreaks of violence. Hate campaigns exposed the dirty politicking below the surface image of stability, and led to a sharp deterioration in inter-ethnic relations, which were already strained in the republic.

The federal presidential elections, which were not regarded as having an impact on local politics, were subject to widespread fraud.[14] International observers were present only once, when the OSCE mission monitored the presidential and parliamentary elections in Chechnya in January 1997. They decided that the elections 'reflected the free will of the republic's eligible voters'[15] and thus avoided the 'free and fair' issue. Nevertheless, the election of a parliament in Chechnya proved a complicated task, as only four candidates gained more than half of the votes in the first round.

Elections across the region to republican and local bodies are viewed as serious and provoke much passion. They are normally held in an atmosphere of acute political rivalry and often feature intimidation of candidates and a number of fatal casualties, with contending groups mobilizing armed support. The present challenge in Dagestan and Chechnya is the merging of the political and criminal worlds, with elections providing a chance for candidates with criminal records, or those widely believed to be engaged in criminal activity, to gain public office. In June 1996 Dagestan passed the Law on Local Government, as the republican authorities were desperate to stop those suspected of links with the criminal world from entering public politics. The Dagestani State Council ruled that all nominated candidates were to be approved by the State Council before official registration. The republican Constitutional Court overruled this provision.

The last issue regarding electoral practices concerns elections in the areas of contested sovereignty and eligibility to vote. In these areas the basis of electoral registration is normally unclear. In North Ossetia the Ingush refugees who fled the republic were encouraged to vote in the January 1998 elections, and the 11,000

[13] Vladimir Abuzov, 'Konflikt v Karachaevo-Cherkessii obostryayetsya', *Nezavisimaya gazeta*, 24 February 1998.
[14] Michael McFaul and Nikolai Petrov, eds, *Politicheskii al'manakh Rossii*, volume 2: *Sotsial'no-politicheskiye portrety regionov* (Moscow: Moscow Carnegie Center, 1998).
[15] *Current Digest of the Post-Soviet Press*, vol. XLIX, no. 4, 1997.

Ingush who took part in the elections were said to have voted for Dzasokhov.[16] In Chechnya the DPs who fled during the fighting were not allowed to vote outside the republic and were required to come back to Chechnya if they wanted to participate in the January 1997 elections. Many were afraid to do so without security guarantees. Although their vote would not, perhaps, have altered the outcome, this cast a shadow over the whole elections. Polling stations close to the borders with Dagestan and Ingushetia were open, and DPs were encouraged to vote there.

Parties

The embryonic party system broadly follows the pattern of Russian politics apart from in Chechnya, where rival groups are engaged in party-building.[17] The Communist Party, as elsewhere in the Russian Federation, has organizational unity and is active at a grassroots level, but does not have influential leaders with any credible chance of being voted into senior office. Communist candidates do not generally stand for the republic elections as party nominees. The party's activity is at its peak during elections to federal bodies. In the federal elections the communist vote has been high in the North Caucasus[18] for three reasons: the conservatism of the population, the war in Chechnya and the chauvinist attitude towards Caucasians in the rest of Russia. President Aleksandr Dzasokhov of North Ossetia is a member of the Communist Party of the Russian Federation and is still registered for party purposes in Moscow, but he rejected the support of the local branch of the Communist Party during the North Ossetian presidential elections. He wanted to be regarded as a national leader, and not a Communist nominee.[19]

To sum up, the present development of political institutions in the North Caucasus has demonstrated some progress in introducing competitive elections and drafting legislation, but it is characterized by the lack of a recognized hierarchy of political accountability. The constitutions provide only the form and shape of government, and there is no consensus among the elites and the population at large on how the republics should be ruled.

[16] 'President Severnoi Ossetii izbran v pervom ture', *Nezavisimaya gazeta*, 20 January 1998.
[17] Chechnya even acquired a fascist party, Nokhchi, founded in 1997, and headed by Shirvani Pashaev, see *NG-Regiony*, 9, 1998, p. 6, in Russian.
[18] Dagestan: 50.8% of the electorate in the 1993 parliamentary elections voted for Communists, 63.3% voted for Zyuganov in the 1996 presidential elections; North Ossetia: 32.9% voted for Communists in 1993, and 51.7% in 1995; 62.1% voted for Zyuganov in 1996. Figures for Zyuganov are taken from the first round of the 1996 presidential elections – the second round was subject to fraud.
[19] There are three communist parties in North Ossetia: the North Ossete branch of the Communist Party of the Russian Federation, the North Ossete VKPB (Bolshevik) party and the Social Justice Party.

20

Power

To an outside observer, and indeed for the republican populations themselves, it is unclear where the locus of power lies. In the words of an elderly Balkar deported as a child to Kazakhstan: 'You ask who holds the power now? Have you ever seen a flock of sheep herded? There are two shepherds who direct the movement of the sheep. Imagine now that the shepherds are gone and the sheep left to their own fate – what would they do? This is what power is today.'[20]

One potential reference point is local tradition. However, traditional Caucasian institutions such as councils of elders and local conflict resolution practices survive only insofar as they legitimize decisions made elsewhere, otherwise their role is reduced to mediation in village disputes.[21] In the conflict between tradition and modernity the most convenient option normally prevails. What has survived in the North Caucasus is a traditionalist mentality in family and neighbourhood relations and a conservative outlook in political practices. The national movements, which appealed to the traditional beliefs and values, in reality practised modern, radical politics. They organized rallies, competed for electoral mandates, sought to alter legislation, issued publications, appealed to the courts about violations of their rights by the authorities and campaigned on TV. At the same time the old communist *nomenklatura*, which stood for modern values such as women's participation in politics, continue to act in a Soviet, conservative way.[22]

The reference point for the North Caucasian leaderships was the previous system of Soviet rule. While the communist regime did not provide liberty, it provided authority. In the North Caucasus, with the exception of Chechnya, the political landscape is dominated by the symbols of communist nostalgia and there is an impression that the old system still exists: representatives of the old *nomenklatura* hold senior offices, practice the same management style and attempt to use the same leverage as before. But since the old central authority has gone, power relations inside the elites and between leaderships and societies are no longer predictable and are not supported by the coherent distribution of punishments and rewards. Therefore, despite the desire of the republican authorities to govern in the Soviet way, they lack both the legitimacy and the coercive power to do so.

The gap between formal and informal ways of conducting politics is evident in every part of the CIS, but the size of the gap in the North Caucasus is the most

---

[20] Anna Matveeva, 'Caucasus on the Rocks', *Transitions* 5:11, November 1998, p. 80.

[21] Discussions in the Untsukul *raion* administration of Dagestan in April 1997 revealed that even the local land disputes are resolved only by the *raion* administration, and traditional mechanisms for resolution were discouraged. The use of elders from mountain villages by Djohar Dudayev in Chechnya to rally support for the regime met with widespread ridicule by the urban population.

[22] On tradition and modernity see Elena Bitova, 'Traditsionalizm i problemy ustoichivosti federativnykh otnoshenii', in J. Azrael, E Pain, N. Zubarevitch, eds, *Evolyutsya*, pp. 227–40.

significant. In societies driven by ethnic and clan loyalties, a process of fragmentation, rather than consolidation of power, is evident. Access to power is relatively easy; it comes in many forms and in small quantities, is easily gained and easily lost. The boundaries between political and economic power are blurred, with many politicians exploiting their positions to benefit from economic restructuring. Neither law nor convention defines political practices. The decision-making processes are opaque, giving rise to uncertainty and unpredictability in government, and in these circumstances informal arrangements are easily made.

One feature of these new arrangements is an increased reliance on informal ethnic networks and regional groupings.[23] Such groupings normally have control over a certain economic asset and are headed by powerful individuals, some of them former *nomenklatura*. The way these assets are being controlled, the dynamic of the relationship between the informal leaders and the rank-and-file and often the very nature of these assets remain obscure – many of them are in the illegal economy and data on them are circumstantial. Yet an understanding of their dynamics is the key to penetrating the real decision-making process in the North Caucasus.

These resources broadly fall into the following categories:

- *Control over the distribution of federal subsidies.* There is little separation of institutional interests from the interests of individuals who head these institutions. The budgets of the North Caucasian republics are heavily subsidized and in the case of Chechnya economic resources are being channelled to the republic to compensate for the war damage. As a result, significant sums are allocated to the republican budgets, and those branches of the governments (such as finance ministries) which control the allocation of money hold powerful economic leverages. Funds are further distributed to the heads of local administrations, putting such officials in a strong position, or they are given to targeted federal programmes. The local leaderships also have a stake in emphasizing instability in the republics in order to be able to manipulate Moscow into continuing to provide them with financial support.
- *Initial capital in 1992–3 coming from bank fraud* (the famous operations with bank *avizo*[24] carried out by Chechens and Dagestanis in 1992, machinations during the 'voucher' privatization of state assets and extortion).

---

[23] *Teips* in Chechnya, ethnic groups in Dagestan, valleys (Digor, Alagir, Tagaur and Kurtatin) in North Ossetia play an important role in their formation.

[24] Avizo are promissory notes. By bribing bank officials or forging *avizo* it was possible to get a spurious slip of paper in one part of the former Soviet Union and cash it in another for huge amounts of money. One Chechen gang netted 60 billion roubles (then worth $700 million) in 1992, according to Carlotta Gall and Thomas de Waal, *Chechnya: A Small Victorious War* (London: Pan Books, 1997), p. 131.

- *Benefits from porous borders and from tax-free trade.* The establishment of the formal border between the Russian Federation and Georgia and Azerbaijan created conditions for unregulated export–import operations, corruption among the border guards and ample opportunity to smuggle goods from the states to the south into mainland Russia. Such trade, especially in Dagestan,[25] Chechnya and North Ossetia, made those who organized, financed and helped to protect the larger operations extremely powerful. The creation of a free economic zone in Ingushetia enabled these individuals to avoid taxation. The largest benefits probably came from the arms trade.
- *Trade, economic resources and housing rights in the region's capitals.* The position of mayor of a capital city is often a powerful one. Said Amirov (Makhachkala), Stanislav Derev (Cherkessk), Mikhail Shatalov (the Russian mayor of Vladikav-kaz, an irritant to the Ossete nationalists) have all emerged as extremely powerful individuals capable of maintaining a firm grip on power in their respective cities. Many of them are believed to have their eye on supreme political authority.
- *Control over local production.* Although local economies officially produce very little, lucrative trade in contraband petroleum products from Chechnya is rampant. Illegal alcohol production in North Ossetia, Kabardino-Balkaria and Karachaevo-Cherkessia, and smuggling black caviar and sturgeon in Dagestan, all bring substantial income.

In Dagestan the formal elite, in its quest to secure power at all costs, became a hostage to informal power networks. In order to secure the Avar vote in favour of abolishing the restriction on his term in office, the Chairman of the State Council Magomedali Magomedov (a Dargin) entered into special deals with Avar strongmen who used the opportunity to achieve their own goals.[26] As a result, the formal leadership was increasingly manipulated by new criminal elites.

Chechnya represents an extreme case of power fragmentation. The internal order can be described as anarchy, with different armed self-governing groups controlling their own territories and contesting central government, and each other, by force. The *teip* system, reinforced by the war, is tearing the state apart. Each military commander emerged as a political authority and a law in himself. None of the Chechen authorities' attempts to integrate them into any kind of order or suppress

[25] The bridge over the Samur at Yarag-Kazmalyar is known as the Golden Bridge.
[26] One of the Avar 'strongmen' Magomed Magomedov, the head of the Kyzylyurt local administration and a prominent local businessman, threatened Prime Minister Khizri Shikhsaidov that he would bring some 1,500 Avar militants to ensure the constitutional order. The matter was quickly settled by satisfying his request: Magomedov's crony was appointed mayor of Kyzylyurt, and the popularly elected mayor was transferred to an insignificant position in Makhachkala.

paramilitary groups by force have had any effect. It is highly unlikely that the present government will have enough power to bring the rival armed factions to order. It seems that the republic will disintegrate into complete chaos, and either the present leadership will initiate a crackdown on armed groups and fall victim to its own assertiveness, as attempts on President Maskhadov's life showed, or it will become a hostage to them. As none of the factions have enough power to suppress all the others, internal turmoil is likely to be exacerbated.

Ideology and legitimacy

Governments are regarded as legitimate if they can provide protection, economic welfare and social justice. In discussing legitimacy it is worth looking not only at whether the authorities' actions follow any established set of rules, but also at whether any coherent rules have emerged. The rulers are also seen as legitimate if they adhere to core national values which are reflected in ideologies – a set of values needed to provide a code of conduct and to justify why the population is required to make sacrifices for certain ends.

Ideology

The collapse of communism left an ideological vacuum which politicians in the North Caucasus have attempted to fill in various ways. One option was an appeal to the glorious past – enlightened aristocratic rule for the Kabardins and Circassians, Caucasian Albania for the Lezgins, free tribal communities for the Chechens and the Imamate of Shamil in Dagestan and Chechnya. These proved useful in terms of image-making and provided communities with a myth of a Golden Age. But there is not enough in these premodern structures to satisfy the criteria for legitimization today.

The predominantly mono-ethnic republics, such as Chechnya, North Ossetia and Ingushetia, managed to foster ideological zeal based on politicized ethnic consolidation. Nevertheless, the struggle for a national cause was not sufficient to hide economic issues and does not address the sub-national divisions in these societies. In other republics half-hearted attempts to promote ideologies of inter-ethnic accord, pursued by the representatives of the majority groups, have not met with much success. In Kabardino-Balkaria, the constitution refers to the 'multi-national people of Kabardino-Balkaria' as an 'integrated civic community' without mentioning 'the Kabardin people' or 'the Balkar people', thus provoking resentment among Balkar ideologists.[27] Islam is potentially a unifying ideology which could cut across the

[27] Khaji-Murat Ibragimbeili, 'O narodnom federalisme i nekompetentnosti', *Nezavisimaya gazeta*, 6 February 1998.

24

ethnic and clan divisions. It is no surprise that Islamic ideology is promoted in Chechnya in an effort to hold society together, though the prospects for success look bleak so far.

Legitimacy

While the formal institutions of democratic government are installed in the majority of cases, what is absent is the democratic process and the values which accompany it. The definition of democracy in terms of elections is a minimal definition. A society could choose its political leaders through democratic means but they might not exercise real power. What in the end undermines the regimes in the North Caucasus is their failure to operate effectively and their continuing inability to provide welfare, prosperity, equity, justice, domestic order and external security.[28] The leaderships are widely regarded as corrupt and their policies as benefiting narrow interests. Although societies do not want to be ruled in the present way, there is no vision of how they should be ruled, and the existing alternatives seem worse. The fact that the old *nomenklatura* is still in power with all its drawbacks is regarded as a better option than domination by the new criminal elites. Nostalgia for authoritarian rule is a widespread popular sentiment, but has no support in practical political reality.

Prospects for stability

The North Caucasian republics appear no more stable now than at the time of the Soviet break-up and further destabilization cannot be ruled out. The policies of the current governments consist of short-term measures to prevent immediate disasters and are motivated more by the apprehension of unwelcome developments than by a proactive stance. The fear of loss of power precludes the leaderships from addressing issues of governance and pursuing long-term policies which could address the fundamental causes of existing problems.

Prospects differ in individual republics, with the western republics appearing more stable than those further eastwards. Adygeia is politically incorporated into Krasnodar *krai* and the old elites in power in both places continue the same relationship, but with less regard for the centre. Karachaevo-Cherkessia seems to be following the Dagestani pattern of destabilization along ethnic lines and violent rivalry among the various groups for power and money which was prompted by the 1999 presidential elections. Kabardino-Balkaria has found an uneasy equilibrium for the time being. Prospects in North Ossetia seemed more hopeful since Dzasokhov's election, but the wave of terrorism and periodic aggravations of the Ossete–Ingush

[28] Samuel Huntington, *The Third Wave: Democratization in the Late Twentieth Century* (Norman and London: University of Oklahoma Press, 1991).

conflict have prevented the government from addressing the social and economic problems facing the republic. Ingushetia is caught between the unresolved conflict with North Ossetia on the one hand and the spillover of instability from Chechnya on the other; and the republican leadership has limited room for manoeuvre. Meanwhile the euphoria over Chechnya's victory against Russia faces the test of the current harsh realities. Dagestan may be heading in the same direction with internal feuds, a breakdown of law and order, increasing fragmentation and a weak government paralysed in the face of formidable challenges.

3 ISSUES OF CHANGE AND INSTABILITY

Security considerations, fears of instability and competition for power drive politics in the North Caucasus. The local leaderships find these factors so alarming that they block out all the other problems, and tend as a result to be paralysed by potential conflicts or to become hostages to them. The cross-border dynamics with the states to the south (Georgia and Azerbaijan) and regions to the north (Krasnodar and Stavropol *krais*) are also largely security-driven. Moreover, all the activities of non-regional actors are regarded as attempts by external powers to get involved in local conflicts and to use them to gain influence.

There are at least 20 actual or potential disputes in the North Caucasian region.[1] The factors leading to these conflicts appear to be:

- the absence of law and order, weak governance, the rise of local militias and widespread crime;
- ethnic rivalry for access to power and control of scarce resources;
- aspirations for homeland formation among peoples who were denied territories or forcibly deprived of them in the Soviet period;
- separatist tendencies to break from the Russian Federation and calls for integration of the current North Caucasian republics into new territorial formations;
- religious, particularly Islamic, mobilization for political ends;
- the domino effect of instability and conflict spreading from one location to another.

Conflicts between republics

The Ossete–Ingush conflict

The Ossete–Ingush conflict, the only incidence of large-scale inter-communal violence within the Russian Federation, erupted in 1992 over the issue of the jurisdiction of the Prigorodny *raion*, an area from which Ingush were deported in 1943. The *raion*, historically Ingush territory, was populated by the Cossacks from the 1820s to the 1920s, when the Cossacks were deported and the Ingush returned. After the Ingush

[1] Arthur Tsutsiev and Lev Dzugayev, *Severnyi Kavkaz: Istoriya i granitsy, 1780–1995*, Vladikavkaz: Centre of Ethno-Political Studies of North Ossete 'Reforma' Foundation, 1997.

returned in 1957 from the Soviet deportation, Prigorodny remained a part of North Ossetia. The Ingush made every effort to return to the territories they regarded as their historical homeland, but faced problems obtaining *propiska* (residence permits).[2]

The Ingush justify their claim to Prigorodny *raion* by the decision of the USSR Supreme Soviet adopted in November 1989 and by Articles 3 and 6 on territorial rehabilitation of the Law on the Deported Peoples adopted in April 1991.[3]

Violence erupted in October 1992 and within a few days Russian federal troops intervened on the North Ossetian side to drive the Ingush out of the republic.[4] Since then major violence has been avoided, but tensions were aggravated in summer 1997, when Ingushetia's President Aushev appealed to the Russian leadership to introduce direct presidential rule in Prigorodny. In response meetings in North Ossetia called for the recreation of self-defence units, and the North Ossetian President Galazov threatened that his republic would break away from rule by Moscow. The conflict widened with the threat by Chechen leaders that if the North Ossetian leadership could not bring peace to the republic, they would be prepared to dispatch an armed unit to restore constitutional order.[5]

Since then official relations have improved. On 15 October 1997 a Programme of Joint Action by the State Bodies of the Russian Federation, the Republic of North Ossetia-Alania and the Republic of Ingushetia was signed to facilitate refugee return and improve local morale. The legal relationship is determined by a Treaty Regulating Relations and Cooperation between the Republic of North Ossetia-Alania and the Republic of Ingushetia, signed in September 1997. The Ossetian side has abolished one law and three pieces of legislature which obstructed repatriation. The constitution of Ingushetia still contains Article 11, which insists on 'the return of the territory which Ingushetia was illegally deprived of'. This article contradicts federal legislation and the Ossetian side could appeal to the Federal Constitutional Court to abolish it. But the existence of such a provision equally serves the interests of those Ossete nationalists who want to paint an image of the Ingush as aggressors.

Dzasokhov's election to the North Ossetian presidency was welcomed by the Ingush side, not least because he is not associated with the conflict. He has made

[2] By 1992 the Ingush constituted 5 per cent of the republic's population.

[3] The Ingush deputies to the Supreme Soviet were among those who lobbied heavily for the law. The North Ossete deputies, including Aleksandr Dzasokhov, seldom attended the sittings of the Supreme Soviet and failed to take part in the debate.

[4] The 1992 violence claimed 583 lives, 350 of them Ingush, 192 Ossetes; 261 are still missing (208 of them Ingush) according to Aleksandr Dzadziev's calculations, using data supplied by the Operational Department of the Office of the Russian Federation Presidential Representative in the Republics of North Ossetia-Alania and Ingushetia, and also data from the North Ossete Ministry of Interior. Alexandr Dzadziev, 'Ossetino-Ingushskii konflikt: sovremennoye sostoyaniye', material submitted for the *Bulletin* (Moscow), Summer–Autumn 1997, pp. 1–2.

[5] Aleksandr Dzadziev, 'Novyi vitok napryazhennosti v zone Ossetino-Ingushskogo konflikta', *Bulletin* 5:16, December 1997, p. 39.

efforts to put some political weight behind the repatriation programme, and to improve the psychological atmosphere. However, when repatriation changed from being a political slogan into an imminent reality, the fragility of the leadership dialogue became apparent. Popular resistance on the Ossetian side intensified, while the Ingush grew increasingly impatient. This led to a wave of kidnappings and killings in summer and autumn 1998 and a general deterioration of the security situation, as well as a breakdown in the dialogue established by the elites.

The Ossete–Ingush conflict was the first test of the federal authorities' conflict management skills. In October 1992 a special federal structure – the Interim Administration in the State of Emergency Zone – was created,[6] and its head given the rank of deputy premier. When the state of emergency was abolished in September 1996, the Interim Committee was transformed into the Office of the Presidential Representative. This office has undertaken measures to facilitate dialogue among the elite and confidence-building.[7]

The Ingush appear to be the net losers in the conflict, and the essence of their present campaign is restoration of the status quo, i.e. return to areas of settlement as of 1992. The main obstacles to repatriation are:

1. acute ethnic tensions. The degree of ethnic resentment between communities has not diminished and elite dialogue has yet to be transformed into grassroots support. The slogans 'co-existence with the Ingush is impossible' on the Ossetian side, and 'we want reconstruction of the territorial integrity of Ingushetia within the 1944 borders' on the Ingush side remain highly popular.

2. the unsatisfactory pace of return of DPs. Neither side is happy with this.[8] The Agreement on Measures on DP Return was signed in Kislovodsk in March 1993, but the Ingush side blames the Galazov leadership for lack of commitment to its implementation.[9]

3. weapons proliferation.[10]

4. refugees from South Ossetia,[11] 9,000 of whom live in the houses of the Ingush in Prigorodny.

5. the absence of credible security guarantees for the Ingush, who doubt the capacity of the North Ossetian police forces to protect them effectively.

[6] In 1995 it became the Interim Committee for the Elimination of the Consequences of the Ossete–Ingush Conflict.

[7] Office of Presidential Representative, 'Deyatel'nost' polnomochnogo predstavitelya Presidenta RF', in *RSO-A i RI*, no. 1, Vladikavkaz/Nazran, 1998.

[8] The Ingush consider it too slow, the Ossetes too rapid.

[9] Timur Matiev, 'Pravda pobezhdayet ne tol'ko v skazkakh', *Ingushetia*, 31 March 1998.

[10] In 1997 alone the Russian Federation Rapid Reaction Regiment of the Interior Ministry discovered 460 light weapons held by the population in the conflict zone.

[11] In December 1997 there were 37,700 refugees in North Ossetia, including 28,100 from Georgia, according to the North Ossete Migration Service, 1998.

Chechnya/Dagestan: integrative and separatist tendencies

The conflict in Chechnya has developed from a national into a regional security problem. Its effects are felt across the North Caucasus, but primarily in Dagestan. Although Dagestan remained calm during the fighting in Chechnya, the postwar situation has brought new dangers and the most serious conflict potential lies in the tensions between the two republics.

Since the war ended, the Dagestani authorities have feared the potential dramatic impact of Chechen independence on Dagestan. This fear has been exacerbated by postwar developments. Russian troops have been withdrawn from Chechnya into Dagestan, and the border is no longer properly guarded, enabling criminal gangs from Chechnya and other armed groups to enter Dagestan.

Subsequent developments have shown that internal turmoil in Chechnya, with blood feuds and a struggle for power forging alliances and enmities across the North Caucasus, has proved even more destabilizing for Dagestan than the straightforward conflict between Chechnya and Russian federal power. Current causes of instability include violence in border areas and territorial claims pursued by the Chechen leaders; links between Islamic radicals in Chechnya and in Dagestan; tensions among the local Chechen population in Dagestan; and the militarization of Dagestan.

Official relations between Djohar (in Russian Grozny) and Makhachkala are poor, although the Dagestani authorities have tried to initiate dialogue between the two and the People's Assembly of Dagestan established inter-parliamentary relations with the Chechen parliament in January 1998. The main obstacle is the Chechen leadership's reluctance to sign the Treaty on Friendship and Cooperation, drafted by Dagestan in November 1996. The Chechens argue that whereas Chechnya is an independent state, Dagestan is a subject of the Russian Federation and can sign a bilateral agreement only with an individual district of Chechnya, not with the Chechen government. This did not prevent Chechnya from signing similar treaties with Stavropol *krai*, Tatarstan and Bashkortostan, however. The Dagestani position is that Dagestan has already signed similar treaties with Azerbaijan and Kazakhstan.

Calls for the unification of Chechnya and parts (or all) of Dagestan were heard in Chechnya in 1997. The Islamic Nation movement, founded in Djohar in August 1997 at a congress of Chechen and other North Caucasian delegates, declared as its proclaimed goal the creation of an Imamate, a state formation incorporating all the lands unified by Shamil in the nineteenth century. The former First Deputy Prime Minister of Chechnya, Movladi Udugov, who led the movement, suggested that the territories of Dagestan populated by ethnic Chechens should join the first independent state in the North Caucasus. Nadirshakh Khachilayev, the chairman of the Union of Muslims of Russia and a Lak from Makhachkala, expressed his support for the concept of an independent Dagestan and for unification.[12] The other religious figure campaigning

---

[12] 'Chechnya Repeats Territorial Claims on Dagestan', *RFE/RL Newsline* 1: 182, 18 December 1997.

for unification on Islamic grounds was Ahmad Akhtaev, who founded the All Union Islamic Renaissance Party in 1990.

Udugov put forward their aims at a roundtable discussion with the Dagestani authorities in December 1997 where he described Dagestan as a Russian colony and suggested that the revival of the peoples of the Caucasus would be impossible without decolonization. The Chechen proposals were:

1. The creation of a Congress of Peoples of Chechnya and Dagestan, which would have legislative powers. This initiative mirrors the creation of the Chechen National Congress in 1991 which declared itself the only legitimate authority in Chechnya and became a vehicle for separation from Russia.
2. The establishment of a joint border patrol and the creation of a Caucasian Interpol.
3. Adherence to *sharia* laws in mutual relations, and use of the *sharia* justice system to try criminals from both sides.

Despite opposition by Dagestani officials in 1997, another meeting took place in Djohar in April 1998. This was chaired by Shamil Basayev, the acting prime minister of Chechnya, who declared the unification of Dagestan and Chechnya the ultimate goal of the new organization.[13] The Dagestani authorities and other influential leaders (none of whom attended the meeting) responded with a joint declaration protesting against the congress and its resolutions.[14]

In the eyes of the Dagestani authorities, the entire Chechen leadership is pursuing a policy of territorial claims, irrespective of their official stance. As Magomed Tolboev, then Secretary of the Dagestani Security Council, observed: 'although Grozny has not made any formal demand for Dagestani territory to be transferred to Chechnya, there is little doubt that, in reality, the Chechen leadership sees our republic as potentially its own territory'.[15]

Dagestani–Chechen relations are complicated by the issue of the *Chechentsy-Akkintsy*, who live in lowland Dagestan on the border with Chechnya. In 1944 they were deported to Central Asia along with other Chechens, and since their return they have aspired to resettlement in their historical homelands in Novolak and Khasavyurt

[13] Basayev was proclaimed an Emir of the joint state formation. The Congress included 26 members, 13 from each side. Only three of the 13 members were representatives of the authorities; the others represented public movements.

[14] Apart from the official authorities, the declaration was signed by the leaders of Lak, Avar, Nogai, Lezgin, Tabassaran and two Kumyk national movements, the Spiritual Board of the Muslims of Dagestan, local branches of Russia's Democratic Choice, the Communist Party, Our Home is Russia and others. See 'Dagestantsy serdyatsya na sosedei', *Nezavisimaya gazeta*, 19 May 1998. The Union of Muslims was the only large organization which sent its representative to the Congress.

[15] Igor Rotar, 'Dagestan on the Brink of War: Moscow and Grozny Fight for Influence in the Republic', *Prism* 3: 17, part 2, October 1997.

raions and to restore Aukhov *raion*. These lands, however, are now occupied by Laks and Avars who were forcibly resettled in these territories from the mountains. Tensions centre around the disputed villages of Leninaul and Kalininaul and the question of resettlement of the Laks and Avars should they be persuaded to move from the villages.[16]

These disputes have been recently overshadowed by Dagestani suspicions about where Chechentsy-Akkintsy loyalties lie.[17] These fears are not groundless – the Chechentsy-Akkintsy voted *en masse* in the 1997 Chechen presidential elections. Basyr Dadaev, the leader of the Chechentsy-Akkintsy, has frequently asserted Chechen historical claims to the entire region. Meanwhile, tensions between Chechens and Avars in Khasavyurt *raion* have been particularly acute following the local elections in April 1997, which were won by an Avar. As a result the position of moderate Dagestani Chechens, who would prefer to be dissociated from the developments in Chechnya, has worsened. If abductions and looting from across the border cannot be stopped, the Dagestani Chechens could become victims of spontaneous violence from other Dagestani groups, as nearly happened in January 1996 at the time of Salman Raduyev's raid on Kizlyar.

Sources of instability within the region

Law and order vacuum

The loss of security is felt at the individual level. In the words of Magomedali Magomedov, 'no one can consider themselves safe'.[18] Political terrorism, assassination attempts and kidnappings have become everyday occurrences in the North Caucasus, and crime has escalated. The rate of armed crimes grew fourfold in 1997.[19] At present, the region rates highest in the Russian Federation for violent crime and terrorist acts. According to Anatolii Kulikov, ex-Interior Minister of the Russian Federation, every ninth murder, two-thirds of terrorist acts and 20 per cent of acts of banditry in the Russian Federation are committed in the North Caucasus.[20]

The worst cases of terrorism are in Chechnya and Dagestan. These include the murder of six workers from the International Committee of the Red Cross in Novye

---

[16] The Laks agreed to move to the lands near Makhachkala, but the Kumyks declared these their historical homeland. Moreover, climatic conditions there are very unfavourable.

[17] Rotar, 'Dagestan on the Brink', p. 3.

[18] Magomedkhan Magomedkhanov, 'Riding the Crime Wave', *WarReport* 53, August 1997, p. 14.

[19] According to Russian Deputy Prosecutor-General Vladimir Ustinov, in 1996 there were 34 armed crimes in Stavropol *krai*, and in 1997 this figure had jumped to 1,071; in Krasnodar *krai* the rise was from 202 in 1996 to 1,459 in 1997, according to ITAR-TASS report in English, 11 April 1997.

[20] Anatolii Kulikov's press conference on the results of the Interior Ministry work in 1997, reported in *Nezavisimaya gazeta*, 28 January 1998. Kulikov mentioned that 80% of all registered acts of terrorism on the territory of the Russian Federation take place in the North Caucasus.

Atagi in December 1996, the death of 69 people as a result of the bombing of an apartment block in Kaspiisk near Makhachkala in November 1996 and the execution of four Granger Telecom employees (three Britons and one New Zealander) in December 1998 in Chechnya. In Dagestan in 1996–8 over 40 terrorist acts were committed against political and business leaders: 14 were killed (seven of them members of the Dagestani parliament, including the Minister of Finance). Out of 269 murders registered in 1998, only 58 per cent have been solved.[21]

Kidnappings have become the quickest way to make considerable amounts of money and some areas of the North Caucasus have become strongholds of organized crime. Official figures state that in 1997 in North Ossetia 28 people were kidnapped, in Chechnya the figure was 246, of whom 64 are still being held to ransom.[22] However, most kidnappings of local people go unreported. With weak state authorities, the kidnapping of civilians has become a virtually unpunishable offence unless the victim's family can afford to embark on a vendetta. Hostages are freed without ransom only when local ethnic leaders intervene. Even though the latter often hold official positions, their authority derives from representing ethnic groups, not state structures. All humanitarian organizations have left Chechnya and Dagestan because of rising crime against foreign aid workers.[23]

Such a booming trade in people would not have been possible without cooperation between Chechen and other North Caucasian criminals. Crime cuts across ethnic lines, sharply contrasting with the lack of cooperation between different republics' law enforcement agencies.[24]

The paralysis of law enforcement in the face of growing crime organized mainly around ethnic mafia groupings is a serious problem. None of the North Caucasian authorities have addressed the problem effectively, although Aleksandr Dzasokhov declared it a priority and embarked on a reorganization of law enforcement agencies in North Ossetia. Cooperation between Russian federal and Caucasian republican agencies presents serious problems, particularly in Chechnya. The Dagestani–Chechen border has emerged as the most volatile area of the North Caucasus, sparking public protests such as road-blocks and protest rallies aimed at putting

---

[21] According to the Deputy Interior Minister Vladimir Kolesnikov, reported by ITAR-TASS, 21 January 1999.

[22] According to Magomed Magomadov, the Chechen security service has intelligence information on all the groups which hold foreign hostages, but is refraining from attempts to free them by force, fearing for the hostages' lives, see *Severnaya Ossetia*, 16 April 1998.

[23] Ernst Muehlemann, Chairman of the PACE's special commission on Chechnya, said on his visit to Grozny that some 50 foreign nationals are being held in Chechnya; see Jamestown Foundation, *Monitor* III: 212, 12 November 1997.

[24] On cooperation between Ossetian, Ingush and Chechen gangsters see Per Ilsaas, 'North Ossetia: Kidnappings in the Mountains', *WarReport* 53, August 1997, p. 15.

pressure on the Chechen authorities and the Dagestani government.[25] The Chechen side has proposed the creation of a Caucasian Interpol to consolidate the policing effort and to establish joint border protection units for the border. The Dagestani authorities, however, regard such initiatives as an implicit bid to take over Dagestan's security structures.

Ethnic rivalry

In Karachaevo-Cherkessia ethnic rivalry recently focused on the presidential elections. One presidential contender, the present mayor of Cherkessk, Stanislav Derev, was a Cherkess and enjoyed support from Cherkess, Abazin and Nogais, while Vladimir Semenov, though half-Russian, presented himself as the Karachai candidate. Karachaevo-Cherkessia's first chance to elect the top executive ended in ferocious competition between its two namesake groups and calls for the republic to be partitioned. In an attempt to appeal to the local Russians, the losing side campaigned for the lowland part of the republic, mainly populated by non-Karachai, to be returned to Stavropol *krai*, leaving the mountainous part to its own fate. After considerable political manoeuvring, Semenov was confirmed as the winner of the second round and proclaimed the new president.

Inter-ethnic tension in Kabardino-Balkaria reached a peak in 1992 when attempts were made to partition the republic. Since then the authorities have maintained a system of affirmative action for the Balkar minority and have been able to incorporate the Balkar elite into the governing structures. Other tensions, however, are mounting, as they are everywhere else in the Caucasus. In 1996–7 there were three explosions in Nalchik, capital of the republic; nobody took responsibility, but President Kokov blamed 'Wahhabis' for the action (see below, note 26).

Inter-ethnic tensions place a strain on Dagestan's social stability. There is competition between lowlanders and highlanders over scarce lands. Migration and the concomitant conversion of pasture lands to agricultural use threatens the lowlanders and their traditional economy and way of life. The Nogais and Kumyks are a shrinking minority in their homelands and have claimed that the ethnic group to which a territory historically belongs should be legally recognized as the owner of its land. In their turn, the mountain ethnic groups have argued that their original enforced migration was to lands which were depopulated, and in the cultivation of which they invested considerable effort. In response the Constitutional Court issued a decision that ethnic groups have no rights to own land or allocate its use, this being the responsibility of the state through the People's Assembly.

[25] *Nezavisimaya gazeta*, 19 May 1998.

34

As a result, land tenure is a controversial issue, and is viewed through the prism of various ethnic groups' claims rather than that of individual rights. The Dagestanis voted against land privatization in a referendum in 1992, fearing that the implementation of a successful land division would provoke inter-ethnic tension (the region had no tradition of individual land ownership). Conflicts over land assigned for the use of one ethnic group within the traditional area of another have already led to serious clashes.

Religious mobilization

Perhaps the most significant drive against the authorities comes from Islamic radical groups, who call themselves Salafiyun ('followers of the way of the ancestors') or Muslims of the Jamaat, while the authorities have labelled them Wahhabis. In the current context 'Wahhabism' is a term used loosely by post-Soviet officials to designate any type of Muslim radicalism, often completely unrelated to the Wahhabi sect in Saudi Arabia.[26] Their form of Islam is fundamentalist in its emphasis on a return to canonical Islamic texts, especially the Koran, and the strict observance of 'original' Islamic prescriptions. They do not smoke, drink or shave their beards, and reject state authority, especially restrictions on the possession of arms. Dagestani radicals do not call themselves Wahhabis, but as it is the most widespread local term it will be used in this chapter.[27]

In Dagestan, Kyzylyurt *raion* is regarded as the stronghold of radical Islam, and its influence is also significant in Tsumada, Buinaksk, Khasavyurt and Karabudakhkent *raions* in central Dagestan, and is growing in southern Dagestan. Among the radicals there are representatives of various ethnic groups, such as Dargins, Avars, Kumyk, Lezgins, but no evidence so far that Dagestani Chechens adhere to this form of Islam. Islamic radicalism mostly appeals to young people. The encouragement to carry arms, as well as financial benefits, makes it especially attractive in current circumstances.[28]

The violence involving Wahhabis in Dagestan started in 1994 with a fight between traditionalists and Arab Wahhabi missionaries who subsequently left the republic.[29] During 1995 and 1996 there were several further clashes and the murder of two officials was blamed on radicals. The first conflict between Wahhabis and traditionalists which gained publicity outside the republic occurred in May 1997 in Chabani-

---

[26] Wahhabism proper is a fundamentalist religious movement in Sunni Islam which emerged in Saudi Arabia in the mid-18th century. It was founded by Mohammad Abd-al-Wahhab and was named after him. Wahhabis reject the cult of local saints, as well the authority of elders.

[27] For more on Islam in the North Caucasus see Edward W. Walker, 'Islam in Chechnya', *BPS Caucasus Newsletter*, September 1998, pp. 10–15.

[28] It is rumoured that every new convert receives $500.

[29] Author's interview with Gussein Abuyev, adviser to the Russian Federation presidential representative in the North Caucasus, April 1998.

Makhi. It claimed two lives and resulted in the taking of 18 hostages. This conflict was pacified only after the involvement of Said Amirov, then Dagestani deputy premier, and the despatch of Dagestani Interior Ministry troops.[30]

The link with Wahhabis in Chechnya was established during the Chechen war. The Jordan-born field commander Emir Khattab organized an armed unit based on Wahhabi affiliation where many Dagestanis served. The Dagestani Wahhabis, who fought in the war in Chechnya, returned home determined to build an Islamic state. During 1997 military and organizational support from Chechnya to Dagestani Wahhabis became more manifest, and it is widely believed that certain Arab countries also assisted financially.[31] The Central Front of Liberation of the Caucasus and Dagestan claimed responsibility for an armed raid on a Russian brigade in December 1997. A number of Islamic militants have been trained in the camps in Chechnya and it is believed that at least four camps are operational.[32] One of the Wahhabi leaders, Kyzylvyurt mullah Bagauddin Mohammed, asserted that 'Dagestan can stay within Russia only if the latter becomes an Islamic state'.[33]

It is ultimately difficult to establish the religious credentials of various Chechen warlords. Khattab identifies himself as a Wahhabi, but Salman Raduyev vehemently distances himself from Wahhabism (he and Khattab are enemies). Movladi Udugov, the leader of the Islamic Nation, abstains from public identification with Wahhabis but is widely believed to be one, as is Zelimkhan Yandarbiyev, ex-president of Chechnya.

Raduyev and the leadership of the 'Fighting Squads of Jamaat of Dagestan' established relations with the signing of Treaty on Military Mutual Assistance in December 1997. The Treaty claims that the 'Islamic Jamaat' of Dagestan and Raduyev's 'Army of Djohar' represent forces fighting for a unified independent Islamic state in the Caucasus.[34] Another organization, the Sword of Islam, claimed responsibility for a number of explosions in the disputed Novolak *raion* in 1998, calling on Laks to leave the Chechen homeland. In May 1998 Wahhabis took 50 policemen hostage.

The Dagestani authorities' response has combined punitive and propaganda measures. Initially efforts were made to incorporate Wahhabis into the mainstream debate, and TV discussions between Wahhabis and traditionalists were arranged in May 1997. After the Wahhabis claimed responsibility for violence, Dagestan's policy became less accommodating. In December 1997 the People's Assembly voted in a Law on the Freedom of Religious Confession, which makes it very difficult for the

[30] Enver Kisriev, 'Clash of Faith', *WarReport* 52, June–July 1997, p. 16.
[31] Interview with Gussein Abuyev, April 1998.
[32] Igor Rotar, 'Chast' musulman gotova k gazavatu', *Nezavisimaya gazeta*, 27 January 1998.
[33] 'Organizatory terakta v Buinakske obeshchayut prodolzhit' voinu', *Nezavisimaya gazeta*, 29 January 1998.
[34] 'Raduyev otmetilsya v Buinakske', *Nezavisimaya gazeta*, 3 February 1998.

Wahhabis to register their congregations, build mosques, publish papers or import religious texts. The Dagestani authorities claim external interference and accuse Muslim fundamentalist groups from Kuwait and Saudi Arabia of instigating *jihad* in Dagestan. In response to the proclamation of an Islamic territory by three villages in central Dagestan in August 1998, the republic's authorities threatened punitive measures and issued strongly worded statements. However, after the assassination of Saidmuhamed-haji Abubakarov, Supreme Mufti of Dagestan and an outspoken critic of Wahhabism, the Dagestani leadership resorted to negotiations and reached an agreement with Islamic rebels based on the principle of non-interference.

In the eyes of the Dagestani authorities: 'Wahhabism, although not possessing a wide social base and not being popular among the majority of the Muslim population of the republic, still represents a real and serious threat in reinforcing religious extremism.' They estimated that, although only 5 per cent of the Muslim population were Wahhabi adherents in 1996, a rapid growth was expected.[35] Others argue that the Dagestani authorities fabricate the image of the Wahhabi enemy for their own political ends.[36]

Although radical Islam began in the North Caucasus in Chechnya during the war, Dagestan soon emerged as a stronghold of radical Islam. From here it spread westwards. Wahhabis started to appear in Kabardino-Balkaria, chiefly finding adherents among young men who had recently moved to the cities.[37] President Kokov attributed three 1997 explosions targeted at official buildings in Nalchik to the Wahhabis, but no evidence of their involvement was produced. In Karachaevo-Cherkessia the Wahhabis have not declared themselves publicly, but there are grounds to believe that they exist there.[38]

It is not surprising that social and economic discontent in the region is being expressed in Islamic terms. In the words of a local observer, 'Wahhabism is a social reaction of the desperate rural masses and disaffected youth in the cities, like early Communism'.[39] It is a reaction to the moral decay and lawlessness of the present order, an expression of resentment towards current injustices, an attempt to find a way out. And it is much more effective than traditional Islam in crossing ethnic and clan divisions.

In contrast, official state-sponsored Islam has failed to become a credible agent of civil society which could serve as an intermediary between the authorities and the

---

[35] Information of the Ministry of Nationalities of Dagestan, April 1998.

[36] The day after the Buinaksk raid the head of Dagestani State Council, Magomedali Magomedov, managed to solicit financial and moral support from the Federation Council using the threat from Wahhabis. Some $35 million were subsequently granted. See Nabi Abdullaev, 'Wahhabism: the Real Enemy or Just a Convenient Target for Dagestan's Leadership?', *IEWS Russian Regional Report* 3: 7, 19 February 1998.

[37] Svetlana Akkieva, 'Kabardino-Balkaria: religioznye problemy', in *Bulletin* 6: 17, February 1998, p. 24.

[38] Aleftina Polyakova, 'Wahhabism v importnoi upakovke', in *NG-Stsenarii* 5, 1998, p. 7.

[39] Interview with Enver Kisriev, April 1998, Makhachkala.

population, convey the popular mood to the state actors and speak from a broader humanistic platform. Official Islam in the North Caucasus has been too pliant towards the local leadership. In addition it has engaged in corruption and lacked an independent political stance. For instance, despite popular outrage at the actions of the Russian federal government during the war in Chechnya, the Union of Muslims of Russia and the Spiritual Board of Muslims of Dagestan, along with all well-known Muslim clerics, publicly appealed to people to vote in support of Yeltsin in the 1996 presidential elections.

Formation of local militias

In response to instability in Chechnya and to other security challenges the North Caucasian authorities have resorted to measures they can undertake locally, for example trying to create self-defence forces or, more plausibly, to incorporate the private armed units which already exist into some form of order. In November 1991 the North Ossetian National Guard was created, and a law of October 1992 gave it new powers.[40] President Aushev warned in autumn 1997 that Ingushetia might be forced to form a Wild Division, and in Kabardino-Balkaria Interior Minister Khachim Shogenov put forward the possibility of setting up armed police assistance detachments.[41]

The more tensions on the Dagestani–Chechen border have intensified, the more the need to create local self-defence units has been articulated not only by informal leaders of public movements, but also by heads of local administrations and other officials. This initiative has been encouraged by the fact that the Russian federal armed units, brought from various Russian regions to the republic, have increasingly become targets of terrorist attacks. Not only can Moscow not guarantee the security of civilians in the border areas, but its own security forces need protection.

In November 1997 the Dagestani Security Council adopted a decision to create self-defence units manned by the local population in the areas bordering Chechnya. The implementation of such a proposal would make administration heads the commanders of micro-armies of their own. Gaji Makhachev, the leader of the Imam Shamil Avar National Front and Chairman of Dagneft, claimed in the People's Assembly that in the aftermath of the Buinaksk raid in 1998 Chechen and Dagestani terrorists were chased off by an armed detachment of the Front – the only force capable of opposing terrorism. These developments have aroused fears among other ethnic groups that the self-defence units would in reality be Avar armed formations

[40] In May 1993 the Guard was transformed into the Department for the Protection of the National Economy, but preserved its structure and weaponry and was finally incorporated into the local Interior Forces. A March 1995 treaty put the Interior Forces in the republic under dual federal and republican control.
[41] *Nezavisimaya gazeta*, 29 November 1997.

operating independently of Makhachkala. Violence in the capital in May 1998 demonstrated that the Laks also have their own armed units, in this case led by the Khachilayev brothers.

In January 1998 Anatolii Kulikov made a statement attacking the creation of self-defence detachments, but his dismissal in March 1998 meant his stance was short-lived. The process of legalizing the informal armed structures which emerged to service the new ethnic elites is going ahead in Dagestan and probably in other republics. New armed structures are also increasing the local administrations' control over the villages and towns they govern.[42] There is a danger that such detachments could turn into rogue armed groups, composed along ethnic lines, and that they might come into conflict with one another.

Border zones

Ossetes and Georgia

The conflict between Georgia and South Ossetia is complicated by the uneasy relations between Russia and Georgia. The main issues of contention are Russia's role in conflicts in Georgia, a dispute over the division of the Soviet military heritage and the Russian military presence in the country.

The conflict in South Ossetia remains unresolved. In the Soviet period over one-third of all Ossetes lived in Georgia, where the South Ossetian autonomous *oblast* had existed since 1922. Against a background of rising Georgian nationalism, South Ossetia declared sovereignty in September 1990 and appealed to Moscow for recognition as an independent subject of the USSR. The Georgian government retaliated with the abolition of South Ossetian autonomy. Violence flared up in 1991–2 and led to the expulsion of most of the Georgian population from South Ossetia and to emigration by Ossetes from Georgia's internal regions. A cease-fire was agreed in June 1992 between Presidents Yeltsin and Shevardnadze with the participation of the South and North Ossetian leaderships. At the moment South Ossetia is still separated from the rest of Georgia by peacekeepers. In 1994 an OSCE mission was given a mandate to monitor the operation and facilitate negotiations, which are conducted under Russian auspices.

During the conflict the North Ossetian authorities adopted a cautious stance. The republic's Supreme Soviet did not pass a resolution on unification, although the South Ossetian leadership several times appealed for it to do so. In 1992 the North Ossetian authorities refused passage through its territory to volunteers of the Russian Legion and to a detachment of the KNK intending to fight in South Ossetia.

---

[42] Enver Kisriev, 'Dagestan: legalizatsiya grazhdanskikh vooruzhennykh formirovanii', in *Bulletin* 5: 16, December 1997, p. 27.

The unresolved status of South Ossetia is a burden for North Ossetia. Officially there are 38,011 refugees from South Ossetia and the rest of Georgia in the republic. However, in reality there are many more migrants from across the border who are now registered as living in North Ossetia. South Ossetia is *de facto* gradually being incorporated into the Russian Federation's economic and social space, with transport and energy supplies coming from the north. Although the Georgian government has taken steps to enable the repatriation of DPs, few have been willing to return. Some have made money in cross-border trade, and presently occupy comfortable places in the new market economy. Others benefited by acquiring the property of Ingush who fled (see section on the Ossete–Ingush conflict, above). Far from there being a movement of repatriation, emigration from South Ossetia is continuing.

Lezgins and Azerbaijan[43]

The Lezgin issue is caught up in the uneasy relationship between Russia and Azerbaijan. This relationship is characterized by disagreement over the legal status of the Caspian Sea, Russian military bases in Azerbaijan and the conflict in Nagorno-Karabagh. Azerbaijan, unlike Dagestan, does not acknowledge that the division of the Lezgins by the international border presents a problem.

Some 250,000 Lezgins live on both sides of the river Samur in southern Dagestan while there are 177,000 in northern Azerbaijan. They have been divided since 1860, but only after the break-up of the USSR, when the border with Azerbaijan became international rather than merely administrative, did Lezgins find themselves in the position of a truly divided people.

Azerbaijan's reluctance to join the CIS in 1992–3 and rejection of Russian border guards to help police the Azerbaijani–Iranian border have contributed to a gradual tightening of the Azerbaijani–Russian border regime. The situation was further aggravated by the war in Chechnya. The border with Azerbaijan was closed by Russia in December 1994, and controls and customs were introduced. The official reason was to secure the border against the flow of weapons and foreign mercenaries into Chechnya. The establishment of border controls came as a shock for the local population. In April 1996, under pressure from the Dagestani government, the regime was relaxed and local residents, mainly Lezgins, were allowed to cross the border freely. After signing the Khasavyurt Accords which ended the conflict with Chechnya, the Russian government finally decided to open the border and recruited more local conscripts to serve as border troops. Since 1996 the Dagestani authorities have taken a more proactive approach, exchanging official visits with Azerbaijan,

---

[43] For more detail, see Anna Matveeva and Clem McCartney, 'Policy Responses to an Ethnic Community Division: Lezgins in Azerbaijan', in *International Journal of Minority and Group Rights* 5: 3, 1998.

signing a Treaty on Friendship and Cooperation and supporting efforts at economic cooperation and border delimitation.

Tensions between Lezgins and Azeris began in 1992, but reached a peak in mid-1994, a time of heavy casualties on the Karabagh front and resistance to conscription in the Azerbaijani army. In May that year violent clashes occurred in Derbent, Dagestan, and in June in the Gussary region of Azerbaijan. In Dagestan in 1991 the *Sadval* political movement had called for the creation of an independent Lezgistan. The Dagestani authorities never supported this claim and it was officially rejected in April 1996 at the sixth congress of Sadval. However, the fear of assimilation as a result of what they saw as Azerbaijan's Turkic nationalist policies and the perception of a threat to their survival as a distinct community remain powerful. Unlike other Dagestani ethnic movements, Sadval and its splinter groups are not led by rich and assertive individuals, nor do they enjoy the patronage of a powerful official within the formal political establishment: their direct political influence is limited. A Lezgin splinter group organized a meeting in Derbent in October 1998 on the eve of presidential elections in Azerbaijan to demand the creation of Derbent autonomous region within the Russian Federation, but outside Dagestan.[44]

In September–October 1997 a number of 'sports camps' appeared in Magaram-kent *raion* of Dagestan. Their members were obviously undergoing military training, but nobody was armed and the authorities could not arrest them. The Azerbaijani authorities became alarmed and moved troops to the border, while Dagestan issued the same appeal to the federal government. While various hypotheses spread about the funding and purpose of the camps, none have been substantiated. After the intervention of the republican authorities the camps seem to have disappeared.

The situation was further complicated by the fact that, with the disruption of official economic ties as a result of the war in Chechnya, many illegal opportunities were opened up including arms- and drug-trafficking. Moreover, with relations between the Russian Federation and Azerbaijan frequently tense and suspicious the Lezgins, who were accustomed to belonging to a single Soviet state and political system, find it difficult to split their loyalties between the two new states.

Tension surrounds the Lezgin issue in Azerbaijan, although there are no discriminatory policies against them. The Lezgins' campaign for national and cultural autonomy is vehemently rejected by the Azerbaijani authorities, who drew the conclusion from the Nagorno-Karabagh experience that autonomy is the quickest road to conflict and secession.

[44] *Nezavisimaya gazeta*, 6 October 1998.

41

The Cossacks and southern Russia

Stavropol *krai* shares a common border with four out of the six North Caucasian republics, and the former Cossack *raions* of Chechnya and Karachaevo-Cherkessia have more than once raised the possibility of joining the *krai*. Stavropol *krai* is host to numerous DPs, with every twelfth migrant in the Russian Federation registered there. Given the immigration pressure, in 1995 the *krai* legislature adopted a law on the Status of a Resident of Stavropol *krai*, which stipulated that resident status can be acquired only after seven years' residence in the *krai*; high tariffs for registration were also introduced. In April 1996 the federal Constitutional Court ruled against the law, but the *krai* deputies retaliated with the adoption of a strict Immigration Code, unique in the Russian Federation, which has been applied since February 1997. Resentment of North Caucasians in the *krai* was exacerbated by terrorism in Mineral'nye Vody in 1993–4, hostage-taking in Budennovsk in 1995 during the Chechen war, the spillover of crime from neighbouring Chechnya and immigration. Relations between the Stavropol *krai* population and the authorities and their North Caucasian neighbours, especially Chechens, remain extremely tense.

After the Budennovsk raid protecting the border areas became a priority for the *krai* authorities, and the Cossacks, whose influence is stronger in the southern border-land areas of the *krai*, acquired some support from the administration. Petr Fedosov, the Stavropol Cossack *ataman* (leader) was co-opted as a member of the Stavropol government. The Cossacks campaign for the right to create self-defence units and carry arms, as well as for the return to Stavropol *krai* of the Shelkovskii and Naurskii *raions* of Chechnya, where Russians still live.

The Cossack movement is supervised on the federal level by the Main Directorate of the Cossack Formations under the Russian Federation president. In 1996–7 the federal authorities introduced a measure aimed at incorporating Cossack organizations into the State Register, proposing to transform them from social organizations into state structures, with financial support and tax benefits.[45] The measure elicited complex responses from the Cossacks and split the movement into feuding groups of loyalists and oppositionists.[46] While some welcomed it as an acknowledgment of their role as a bulwark of federal authority in the North Caucasus, others feared that the state authorities would gain overall control of the movement.

The rise of the Cossack movement in Stavropol *krai* and the possible tacit support for it by the *krai* authorities is a cause for concern among the North Caucasian leadership, and relations between Stavropol *krai* and Dagestan are particularly tense.

[45] On the federal policy towards the Cossacks see Vassilii Andreev, 'The Cossacks: a Tribute to History or a Real Political Force in Contemporary Russia?', *Prism* III: 9, 16 May and 13 June 1997.

[46] See Larissa Khoperskaya, V. Kharchenko, 'Kazache dvizheniye v Respublikakh Severnogo Kavkaza', *Bulletin* 2: 13, May 1997, p. 38–40; and 'Kak Kondratenko Kazakov obidel', *NG-Regiony* 2: 5, February 1998.

Cossack patrols have been put on the administrative borders with Chechnya and Dagestan. However, the Cossack movement, internally split and lacking decisive leadership, does not present a credible force capable of military or political undertakings.

Stavropol *krai* is also an arena for Russian nationalist organizations. Lately the Russian National Unity Party, headed by Aleksandr Barkashov, stepped up its activities and organized a conference attended by 450 delegates from Russia's southern regions.[47] Barkashov's supporters have been joined by some of the Cossacks. The demands pursued by these groups include the return to Krasnodar and Stavropol *krais* of the Russian-populated *raions* allocated to the North Caucasian republics in 1957, or the abolition of the North Caucasian republics and the creation of non-ethnic *guberniyas* (provinces), headed by *atamans*.

Prospects for security

While some old conflicts are dormant or on their way towards resolution, new dangers are emerging. The major threats to security come from within the region and are interrelated: the escalating tensions between Chechens and Dagestanis; the rise of Islamic radicalism. Both Chechens and Dagestanis have armed formations and problems between these groups might lead to inter-communal violence. The issue is: who will defend the populations if violence breaks out? After the humiliating defeat of the Russian troops the belief in Russian military strength in the Caucasus has been shattered. It may well be that in the medium term the North Caucasus will emerge as a zone of chaos between the South Caucasian states and the regions of Southern Russia.

[47] BBC Monitoring Service, 6 September 1998, quoting Russian Public TV, Moscow, 5 September 1998.

4 ECONOMIC AND SOCIAL TRENDS

From the geo-economic perspective the significance of the North Caucasus is determined by the transportation links across its territory. Its own productive potential is limited, while its social problems are huge.

Apart from political factors, the situation is aggravated by the occurrence of general problems associated with the post-communist transition at the same time as specific development challenges. These include technical and commercial modernization or migration from the countryside into the towns and from the highlands to the plains. At the same time, the agents that might be expected to respond to these challenges, such as central government or international development organizations, are absent. Meanwhile, economic readjustment has disrupted traditional economic groupings, produced *nouveaux riches* who are not yet absorbed by the existing order and increased the gap between rich and poor.

In contrast to the large and rich *krais* of Southern Russia, the North Caucasian republics are relatively poor in economic potential and possess severe geographical disadvantages. Apart from minerals, they can offer hydrocarbon resources, hydro-electric power and tourism. These are unlikely to be developed in the near future – the North Caucasus is regarded as the least attractive region in the entire country for foreign investors.[1] The significance of its transport routes, however, do create potential for this otherwise neglected area to play a role in developments around the Caspian Sea basin.

Energy resources

In Soviet times Baku and Grozny were major centres for research and the production of equipment for the oil industry. Grozny possessed oil and gas refineries: Grozneftekhim had an all-Union monopoly in aviation petrol and paraffin production and Krasnyi Molot factory specialized in oil equipment. The North Caucasian oil resources were among the first to be exploited by Russia. At the beginning of the century they accounted for 10 per cent of the oil produced in the Russian empire, but on present estimates no more than 100 million tonnes remain.[2]

---

[1] According to Credit Suisse First Boston; Moscow, cited by *The Economist*, 3 January 1998.
[2] Sufficient for 15–20 years at current rates of production.

Oil production peaked in the early 1970s, while the production of natural gas has been in decline since the late 1960s. Oil extraction declined to 3.6 million tonnes in 1992 when over 75 per cent of crude oil for the Grozny refineries came from outside the region. At present, the North Caucasus has lost its prominence as a fuel base. In the early 1990s it accounted for 1.8 per cent of the crude oil and 0.8 per cent of gas production of the Russian Federation.[3]

Today the Chechen government places much hope on oil extraction and refining as a means of revitalizing the economy, but the Caspian Sea oil development and the oil price drop make the prospects bleak. Chechen officials claim that Chechnya's output has increased to 4,000 tonnes per day, but the illegal tapping of pipelines is an acute problem. Stolen oil is either refined into petrol locally, or sold to middlemen in North Ossetia to be refined there. Cheap petrol is on sale throughout the North Caucasus and southern Russia. Obsolete war-damaged and degraded plants hamper the refining industry.[4] Storage facilities were completely destroyed during the war.[5] In March 1995, the Southern Oil Company (YUNKO) was set up by the Russian authorities to manage oil production, refining and transportation in Chechnya. In October 1997 Maskhadov disbanded the company and instead set up four state companies handling production, refining, transportation and marketing answerable to the Chechen president himself.

Most foreign investors have been very cautious in their approach towards oil development in Chechnya and no significant investment has been made, though there has been some interest expressed in the CaucOr project which aims to raise $3 billion for investment projects in the Caucasus, several of them energy-related.[6]

Oil and gas also are of local significance (in 1996 Dagestan produced 354,000 tonnes of oil), but this might change if substantial offshore resources were discovered in the Russian part of the Caspian.[7] This area of the sea was not developed in Soviet times – Western Siberian deposits were much larger, and as this part of the Caspian is

[3] The reconnoitred reserves of oil in the region are in Stavropol *krai* (34%), in Chechnya and Ingushetia (33%), in Krasnodar *krai* (27%), in Dagestan (5%).

[4] According to Jennifer DeLay, editor of *Energy and Politics*. The first refinery was built by the British in the 19th century.

[5] *NefteCompass* 7: 5, 29 January 1998.

[6] From the British side the project is led by Lord McAlpine, the former Treasurer of the Conservative Party; Francis Pike, the executive director of Peregrine Investment Holdings; and Patrick Robertson, the chief executive of the London consulting firm Robertson and Associates. Political support was rendered by President Maskhadov and Baroness Thatcher. Tsezar Shevardnadze and Altai Khasanov, other co-founders of CaucOr, are the nephews of the presidents of Georgia and Azerbaijan respectively; see *Prism* III: 20, part 3, 1997. Among the ambitious plans are hopes to build a pipeline to the Iranian refineries in Tabriz, and a rail terminal and storage facilities for oil products in Sarakhs in northeastern Iran, and to revitalize the Chardzou refinery in Turkmenistan; see *NefteCompass* 7: 8, 19 February 1998.

[7] Russian oil resources in the Caspian were estimated at 1 billion tonnes. However, new deposits discovered in 1998 are believed to contain around 600 million tonnes, see 'Kaspiiskii globalnyi pas'yans', *NG-Sodruzhestvo* 4, 1998, p. 4.

uniquely rich in sturgeon and black caviar there were fears that oil development might pose a threat to its ecosystem.[8] The energy reserves in the Dagestani sector (32,000 km) were estimated at 931 million tonnes of oil equivalent in 1995, of which oil accounted for 313 million tonnes and gas for 618 million tonnes; 181 million tonnes of oil and 540 of gas are located onshore. The most commercially viable deposits are Duzlak, Berekei, Arablyar and Derbent.[9] The Inchkhe–More deposit at 4km depth, located near Izberbash, is the only one for which a tender has been awarded, and the Caspoil joint venture including JKX Oil & Gas Ltd (30.5 per cent), RosKaspNeft (39.5 per cent) and DagNeft (30 per cent) was set up for its development. According to Russian estimates, the reserves of the deposit stand at 9–10 million tonnes of oil and 180 billion cubic metres of gas. Since 1996 Lukoil has started an exploration programme in the northern part of the Caspian shelf. The oil and gas development is supervised from Moscow, and Dagestan has to coordinate its role with the federal Fuel and Energy Ministry. The Dagestani authorities hope to be allowed to retain most of the income in the republic in exchange for a reduction of federal subsidies.

In Dagestan Gaji Makhachev, Chairman of DagNeft, attempted to build a modern infrastructure for the oil industry. He initiated a raid to crack down on illegal refineries and started building an oil refinery in the Makhachkala area of 300,000 tonnes annual capacity with projected expansion of up to 1 million tonnes. Makhachev has already built a fibreglass pipe factory in collaboration with the US firm MG-Corporation (30 per cent share) in Kyzylyurt. This was completed in 1997. Foreign investment in this factory, together with a gas works, accounted for 1 per cent of the Dagestani budget (slightly over $1 million) in 1996. Some 800 million cubic metres of gas per annum is being extracted at present. DagNeft hopes to increase extraction to 1.2 billion cubic metres in 1999, to satisfy the needs of Dagestan.[10]

North Ossetia also possesses modest oil resources, and during his presidency Akhsarbek Galazov managed to obtain federal subsidies to have them developed. The Zamankul deposit (up to 500,000 tonnes production per annum) was pumping crude to Chechnya until 1993, when it became apparent that oil losses through theft were excessive and the work stopped. It is argued in North Ossetia that this amount of oil does not justify the damaging consequences for the environment and reduces Ossetia's potential as a tourist resort. Nevertheless, an oil refinery with a capacity of 15,000 tonnes per annum has already been built, and there are plans to build a further ten to fifteen mini-refineries.

---

[8] Similar concerns are articulated today, see Vyacheslav Zilanov, 'Kaspiiskoe Morye: ryba ili neft'? – Unikal'naya ekosistema regiona nakhoditsya pod ugrozoi unichtozheniya', in *Nezavisimaya gazeta*, 22 August 1997.

[9] Igor Zonn, *Kaspiiskii Memorandum* (Moscow: Russian Academy of Natural Sciences, 1997), p. 63.

[10] Author's interview with Gaji Makhachev, April 1998.

Hydro and gas-generated electric energy is a potentially vast resource, and with the advancing capacities of long-distance transmission, electricity may play an important role in the future. Dagestan leads in this sphere: its Irganai, Chikiyurt and Cherkei power stations have the highest capacity in the North Caucasus. In 1996 Dagestan produced 2,385 million kilowatt hours of electricity.[11] In Soviet times it used to swap electricity with Azerbaijan because the republics had surpluses in different seasons. At present Dagestan supplies electricity to Stavropol *krai* and to Chechnya, but Chechnya is not paying for it. This debt is taken into account by the federal authorities when allocating subsidies to Dagestan.

In other republics medium-scale hydro power projects are under way. In North Ossetia the construction of Zaramag hydro power station (466 MW) has started. It is financed by the federal budget (96 million roubles), and by United Energy System (UES) (70 million roubles). The North Ossetia government decided to take part in financing the project (8 million roubles in 1997), so that the republic could be a shareholder in it as well.[12]

Federal subsidies

The scale of subsidies is hard to determine. According to the official data, 87 per cent of the Dagestan budget was provided by subsidy in 1994, and in 1996 the figure was 71 per cent. In North Ossetia 45 per cent of the republic's budget comes from the federal fund for social support for the regions, but money also comes through direct transfers and through federal investment programmes.[13] According to local observers, the Kabardino-Balkaria budget is 80 per cent subsidy.[14]

Within the Russian Federation Dagestan leads as a recipient of subsidies in absolute rouble terms. Some 5 per cent of the federal fund for social support for the regions ($500 million) is allocated to Dagestan, the population of which is slightly over 1 per cent of the Russian Federation. A further $170 million is channelled towards targeted investment, such as the Irganai hydro power station and the reconstruction of the port at Makhachkala. Apart from that, state pensions are paid out of the federal budget and the transport network (railroads, electricity transmission lines and pipelines) is also financed directly from Moscow. There are also money transfers designed to compensate the region for the losses caused by factors beyond its control,

---

[11] *Sotsial'no-ekonomicheskoye polozheniye Respubliki Dagestan*, Committee for State Statistics of the Republic of Dagestan, Makhachkala, 1997.

[12] Interview with Valerii Balikoyev, Minister of Economics of North Ossetia, April 1998.

[13] According to Balikoyev, 50 million roubles were allocated from the regions' support fund in 1996; in 1997 the figure had increased to 78 million, and the same sum was designated for 1998 (all in 'new' roubles). Interview with Balikoyev, April 1998.

[14] Interview with academician Petr Ivanov, Nalchik, April 1998.

such as inflation and emergencies. It was recently decided that the federal budgetary allocations would be distributed not via commercial banks, as before, but only via a number of centrally approved banks.

The Dagestani authorities use three main tactics in lobbying Moscow: by creating an image of a besieged fortress in need of support; by emphasizing Dagestan's role in Caspian Sea oil transportation; and by highlighting the pressure from Dagestani Communists in the State Duma.[15] In his bid for subsidies Magomedali Magomedov used to appeal directly to Viktor Chernomyrdin, with whom he had a close relationship, and occasionally even had access to Boris Yeltsin. Ramazan Abdullatipov (Nationalities Minister) is the most influential Dagestani in Moscow politics and also lobbied for the republic. Moreover, Magomedov managed to win half of the subsidies in cash allocations, not in tax amnesties.[16] Their attempts to gain the goodwill of Anatolii Chubais, first vice premier at that time, were unsuccessful, however, and the dismissal of Chernomyrdin and appointment of Sergei Kiriyenko were regarded as very unfavourable for Dagestan's chances of winning further subsidies.[17] The current situation is not clear. In 1998 Moscow attempted to shed some light on how subsidies are spent and reduce the allocations, but fears about the rise of Wahhabism encouraged the continuation of the status quo.

Federal programmes are another important undertaking. They are set up to bring investment into strategic areas and to satisfy the development needs of the republics. In some cases they are aimed at the restoration of historical justice, providing compensation and development for the ethnic groups deported during the Second World War, such as the Balkars and Ingush. Since 1994 programmes for socio-economic and cultural development have been approved for all the republics. Programmes are adopted by a combination of presidential and governmental decisions. For instance, Measures for State Support for the Social and Economic Development of Kabardino-Balkaria ($32.6 million was spent in 1997) were adopted by a presidential decree, while the government passed a resolution on State Support of the Infrastructure for International Tourism in Kabardino-Balkaria ($184,000 was spent in 1997).[18]

In North Ossetia a presidential decree on State Support for the Social and Economic Development of North Ossetia until 2000 was signed in October 1994, and a programme to this end was approved in March 1996 by the Russian government. The body in charge of the programme was the Russian Federation Ministry for

[15] This is ironic. The Dagestani authorities struggled against the Communists and supported Nadirshakh Khachilayev in his electoral campaign because he is a Lak. He subsequently claimed that he advocates the interests of the Union of Muslims, not the Republic of Dagestan.

[16] Nabi Abdullaev in *IEWS Russian Regional Report* 3: 13, 2 April 1998.

[17] Nevertheless, Mikhail Zadornov, the Minister of Finance, promised Magomedov in April 1998 that the subsidies would not be cut; see *Argumenty i Fakty*, 15 April 1998.

[18] *Itogi sotsial'no-ekonomicheskogo razvitiya KBR za 1997*, State Committee for Statistics of Republic of Kabardino-Balkaria, 1998.

Nationalities and Federal Relations, while the North Ossetian government was responsible for its implementation. The programme is broken down into 15 projects, including those covering conversion of the defence industries, oil, mineral water, mountains and energy. The programme requires an investment of $7 billion which is broken down as follows:

Federal budget	27 %
Direct investment	24 %
Centralized investment funds	11 %
Non-budgetary funds & credits	23.4%
Republican budget	14 %
Other	0.6%

The objectives of the programme were a reduction of subsidies from 70 per cent to 20 per cent, a five-fold increase in electric energy production, housing for 45,000 DPs and the reduction of unemployment from 7 per cent to 3 per cent.[19] The programme failed to stop the increase in unemployment (the current figure is over 10 per cent), nor did it help to clear the republic's $90 million budget deficit. In fact, North Ossetia continues to receive up to 90 per cent of its budget in federal subsidies and it ranks 86th in consumer capacity in the Russian Federation. Whether financing will continue until 2000 remains uncertain.

Since taking office, President Dzasokhov has chosen what might prove to be more viable tactics. He managed to persuade Boris Yeltsin that most of the revenue generated by customs should stay in the republic and not be transferred to the federal budget. In exchange border posts and customs inspections would be maintained at the republic's expense.

The ability to obtain subsidies depends on good connections in Moscow. As a Deputy Speaker of the Federation Council, Kabardino-Balkaria's President Valerii Kokov is well positioned. His relations with the Moscow political establishment (Chernomyrdin, Kulikov and Yeltsin himself) were instrumental in getting programmes financed. His close ties with Yuri Luzhkov, mayor of Moscow and a likely presidential candidate, may also prove useful in future.

Concerned about the situation in Dagestan, Moscow has attempted to exercise more control over the republic. In September 1997 the federal government adopted a decision for the Economic Stabilization and Development of the Economy of the Republic of Dagestan, according to which $380 million of foreign loans guaranteed by the Russian government were to be allocated to the republic. The programme envisages the creation of five local free economic zones to produce export goods.

The current scale of subsidies is unlikely to continue indefinitely, however. Even when the Federation Council approved the 1998 budget, there were complaints by the

---

[19] Federalnaya Tselevaya Programma, 'Sotsial'no-ekonomicheskoye razvitiye Respubliki Severnaya Ossetia – Alania do 2000 goda', Moscow, 1996.

governors about inequitable distribution to the regions.[20] Mounting social tensions in the Russian regions could make the federal government divert most of the funds allocated for social support to areas where protest might lead to direct political consequences for its own stability.

In spite of the high level of subsidy, the republics' budgets are in deficit. The scale of deficit has only been revealed in North Ossetia, where the gross financial mismanagement of the Galazov administration was discovered after the transfer of power to Dzasokhov. Galazov borrowed $66.4 million from the commercial banks, a sum which is roughly equal to the republic's entire annual budget. The money required to service the debt could have covered the salaries of one-third of the republic's employees in the state sector. In Kabardino-Balkaria the budget deficit was $3.2 million in 1997 and only 49 per cent of revenue was generated in the republic.[21] In 1996 the Dagestani budget was $80 million in deficit and the republic transferred 13.3 per cent of its revenue to the federal budget.[22]

Ingushetia presents a sharp contrast to its significantly more industrialized neighbour North Ossetia. A new capital – Magas – has been built, numerous construction projects are in progress and several other projects to develop consumer industries are already finished. Such intense activity has been possible because Ingushetia made use of the free economic zone status it was allocated in 1994, although the zone was abolished in July 1997 following state losses of about $400.[23] After this Ingushetia became a Zone of Intensive Economic Development, a status which gives fewer privileges than the free economic zone, but still offers substantial benefits. The opposition claims that spending went on grandiose projects, such as a new airport in Nazran, rather than job creation (youth unemployment is estimated at 80 per cent) or the development of the oil sector.[24]

Foreign aid

During the war in Chechnya international and non-governmental organizations rendered humanitarian relief to the population, but development organizations never came to the region. The largest donor at present is the European Union, which announced in October 1997 that it would release 700,000 ecus ($798,000) in humanitarian aid to Chechnya for war victims and for infrastructure projects.[25]

---

[20] *IEWS Russian Regional Report* 3: 11, 19 March 1998.

[21] *Itogi sotsial'no-ekonomicheskogo razvitiya KBR za 1997.*

[22] *Uroven' zhizni naseleniya Dagestana*, State Committee for Statistics of the Republic of Dagestan, Makhachkala, 1997.

[23] 'An Inevitable Fight: Chubais Ends Free Economic Zone in Ingushetia', *The Current Digest of the Post-Soviet Press* XLIX: 28, 1997.

[24] Issa Kostoev interviewed by *Nezavisimaya gazeta*, 'Podvodnye kamni prezidentskoi gonki', 19 February 1998.

[25] *RFE/RL Newsline* 1: 151, 3 November 1997.

Transport infrastructure

Pipelines

Oil transportation is the most important aspect of the transport infrastructure, with competition for routes exacerbating political tensions.[26] Oil transit is the only issue on which Moscow and Djohar have managed to agree since the signature of the 1996 Khasavyurt Accords. The agreement on oil transit was signed in July 1997 between TransNeft (the Russian pipeline company), YUNKO (the Chechen oil company) and SOCAR (the Azerbaijani state oil company). This tripartite agreement was concluded purely on commercial grounds and enabled the parties to stick to their own views on the status of Chechnya.[27] At the time Vice-Premier Boris Nemtsov expressed the predominant view that 'any arrangement would suit if it enables the pipeline to work'.[28] In September, after difficult talks, a transit-fee agreement was concluded between Moscow and Djohar according to which 200,000 tonnes per annum of Azerbaijani oil were to be shipped for a flat fee of $854,000 ($4.27 per tonne).[29] In November 1997 early oil from the Caspian offshore deposits exploited by Azerbaijan International Operating Company began to flow through the Baku–Djohar–Tikhoretsk –Novorossiisk pipeline (less than the 200,000 tonnes has actually been transported),[30] but the agreement was valid only until the end of December. Four months were spent in negotiations before TransNeft and ChechenTransNeft (the Chechen oil pipeline operator) reached a new agreement to send 2.2 million tonnes via Chechnya at $3.58 per tonne.[31]

For Moscow the smooth functioning of the pipeline is crucial in its bid for the northern route for the main export pipeline from the Caspian Sea basin. For the Chechen government the pipeline is the main source of stable income for urgent social needs, and it is apprehensive of any disruptions. The authorities deployed a round-the-clock security force to guard the 153km Chechen stretch of the pipeline against theft and sabotage.[32] Oil transit was put in jeopardy in January 1999 by a fire on the oil well near Djohar, believed to be a result of intra-Chechen competition for ownership of the well.[33]

[26] On oil politics before the war see Elaine Holoboff, 'Oil and the Burning of Grozny', *Jane's Intelligence Review* 7: 6, June 1995, pp. 253–7.

[27] The initial Chechen bid was that it should be included in the agreement as a sovereign country dealing directly with Azerbaijan, and insisted on being paid $20 per tonne of transit, while Russia was getting $15.67 according to the Russian–Azerbaijani agreement of 1996.

[28] *Kommersant Daily* 109, 12 July 1997, cited by Igor Zonn in *Kaspiiskii Memorandum.*

[29] According to Yarikhanov, see *Energy and Politics* 17, part 1, May 1998.The fee included the cost of repairs to the damaged pipeline.

[30] According to Yarikhanov, the remaining oil was shipped in early 1998, when the transit accord had already lapsed; see *Energy and Politics* 14, part 1, April 1998.

[31] *Energy and Politics* 17, part 2, May 1998.

[32] The guards are being paid relatively high wages of $334 per month, according to *Pipeline News* 79, part 1.

[33] Interfax, 20 January 1999.

Tensions and doubts around the pipeline persist. At present the Russian northern route does not have the capacity to transport the amounts of oil (up to 100 million tonnes per annum) which may be exported from the Caspian Sea in the next century. Currently it can transport up to 20 million tonnes annually. During his time as prime minister Sergei Kiriyenko announced that the Russian government was willing to expand the capacity to 30 million tonnes per year, but oil producers in Azerbaijan have been suspicious about TransNeft's commitment to ship Azerbaijani oil on fair terms and on a regular basis.[34] Moreover, Russia possesses only two oil terminals (in Novorossiisk and Tuapse) of 40 million tonnes combined capacity.

A second problem is the disagreement between the Russian and the Chechen authorities which arose over who owns the actual pipeline in Chechnya. Movladi Udugov proposed that the international consortium (AIOC) engaged in exploiting three Azerbaijani Caspian oil fields should lease the Chechen sector of the export pipeline, but Russia rejected this bid as illegal, affirming that the pipeline belonged to the Russian federal government.[35]

The most important factor is Russia's growing perception of *de facto* Chechen independence. Despite the agreement with Chechnya on the northern route for the Caspian Sea oil, the Russian federal authorities are seeking to reduce their dependency on the goodwill of the Chechen government.[36] Hence the idea of a bypass pipeline via Dagestan to transport oil from Azerbaijan to Tikhoretsk in Russia, although Azerbaijan initially dismissed the proposal as not viable.[37] In September 1997 First Deputy Prime Minister Boris Nemtsov announced the intention to build a 312km pipeline with a diameter of 720mm and three associated pumping stations.[38] The US company GP Redd announced that it was willing to finance the construction of the bypass (the idea supported by DagNeft)[39] but the federal authorities ruled in favour of a Russian company. In January 1998 the Russian company Rosneftegazstroi was awarded a $250 million contract to lay a section of pipeline in Dagestan and completion was expected in nine months.[40] The work has not yet started, however, and it appears that the project has been abandoned for security reasons.

[34] *Energy and Politics* 14, part 1, April 1998.

[35] *RFE/RL Newsline* 1: 144, 22 October 1997.

[36] On potential problems see Rajan Menon, 'Treacherous Terrain: the Political and Security Dimensions of Energy Development in the Caspian Sea Zone', *Eurasian Energy, National Bureau of Asia Research*, December 1997, p. 22.

[37] *Inside Central Asia* 190, September 1997. However, the Russian–Azerbaijan contract of January 1996 stipulates that Azerbaijani oil is to handed over to TransNeft on the border in Dagestan, and Russia is responsible for its transit to Novorossisk.

[38] 'Nemtsov Wants Bypass Pipeline Completed by End-1998', *Pipeline News* 77, part 1, November 1997.

[39] According to Makhachev, Redd was prepared to invest $300 milllion. Author's interview, April 1998.

[40] *Energy and Politics* 2, part 2, January 1998.

Gaji Makhachev welcomed the bypass idea. DagNeft officials claim that the bypass could bring Dagestan $30 million a year in transit duties. At present Dagestan gets $0.47 per tonne, while Chechnya gets $3.58.[41] The Dagestani and Ingush authorities (the largest pumping station is located in Ingushetia) have questioned the fairness of such an arrangement, as they do not generate any special revenue out of the pipeline through their territories and hope to renegotiate their own individual deals with Moscow. However, given the present scale of subsidies, the North Caucasian republican authorities do not venture to play pipeline politics with Moscow.

The success of the Dagestan route idea would mean that the pipeline section via Chechnya would become redundant and the republic would not only be deprived of the transit benefits, but also face the reduction of opportunities to export its own oil and receive technical assistance in maintenance of the facilities. As a result the route via Dagestan is potentially vulnerable to terrorist attacks, and the armed raids on Kizlyar (1996) and Buinaksk (1998) demonstrate how easy it is to penetrate Dagestani territory. Khozh Akhmet Yarikhanov, presidential adviser on fuel and energy, warned that 'any attempts by Moscow to bypass Chechnya by building alternative pipelines, transport corridors or power lines are doomed'.[42]

Rail, road and sea communications

Mountainous terrain makes communications in the North Caucasus very difficult and has brought about the region's relative isolation. Several individual republics rely heavily on a single external transportation link. The geographical isolation of the North Caucasus is aggravated by the extreme vulnerability of its transport networks.[43] The principal obstacle is the main Caucasus mountain range, with the only easy passage via the Darial Pass where the Georgian military highway runs, and via the territories lying on the sea coast (Dagestan and Krasnodar *krai*), which have special importance for maintaining links between Russia and the states to the south. The railway connecting Krasnodar *krai* with Georgia is not functioning owing to the unresolved Georgian–Abkhaz conflict and the blockade of Abkhazia. At the moment road transportation is often the only land option in the North Caucasus, but corruption among the numerous agencies which guard the roads (individual republics have their own customs and border guard posts),[44] as well as banditry, reduce the number of those prepared to ship goods in the Caucasus.

[41] Interview with Makhachev, April 1998.
[42] *Energy and Politics* 14, part 2, April 1998.
[43] Larissa Ruban, 'Growing Instability in the North Caucasus: A Major Threat to Russian Regional Security', *Caspian Crossroads* 3: 2, pp. 15–19.
[44] For instance, Kabardino-Balkaria installed customs and border posts on the border with Ingushetia; see *Nezavisimaya gazeta*, 11 February 1998.

Three ports are important for sea communications: Novorossiisk, Astrakhan and Makhachkala. Russia has started to build a new coastal defence infrastructure in Astrakhan, and the Caspian flotilla, originally withdrawn from Baku to Makhachkala following the break-up of the Soviet Union, will be based there in future.

Chechnya is situated at the heart of the transportation node, and infrastructural links have been disrupted since before the war. In the present climate of mutual hostility there is a strong urge in the Russian federal government to bypass Chechnya by constructing alternative links. Thus after a number of years of lobbying by the Dagestani government and with the end of the Chechen war in 1996, Moscow finally constructed a railway to bypass Chechnya and connect Dagestan with Astrakhan.[45] The opening of the border and proper functioning of the railway led to an increase in trade with Azerbaijan, and Russia became Azerbaijan's leading trading partner again.[46] The new rail link started to function in June 1996 but was subsequently the subject of terrorist attacks.[47] Nevertheless, a second railway link is under construction which will connect Budennovsk in Stavropol *krai* via Neftekamsk to Kochubei in Dagestan. This should be completed by summer 1999. Long-distance electric energy transmission lines are also being constructed bypassing Chechnya (Kizlyar–Kochubei–Neftekumsk).

Meanwhile Chechnya is looking for alternative transport links. The only other country with which it shares a border is Georgia. An agreement to build a highway to Georgia was made between Djohar Dudayev and Zviad Gamsakhurdia in 1991. The construction of the Chechen side was completed in 1998, but Georgia is in no hurry to finish its section.

Linkages and alignments

The ideal of North Caucasian integration emerged in the perestroika period and is linked to the short-lived existence of the Mountain Republic in 1921. After nearly ten years attempts to achieve integration based on politicized regional identity have foundered, while ethnic identities have proved to be much stronger. The idea of a pan-Caucasian confederation modelled on the EU,[48] to which Chechens and the Abkhaz aspire, seems quite unrealistic, as well as politically unacceptable for Georgia or Azerbaijan. Given the current political tensions between most of the neighbours in the North Caucasus, regional cooperation is more a slogan than a reality. However, a

[45] The railway is only 78km long, but required the construction of 54 bridges. The bypass was built in eight months.
[46] According to the acting trade minister of Azerbaijan, Farhad Aliev, Russia's share in Azerbaijani trade turnover was 21.1 per cent in 1997, while Iran's was 15.1 per cent, and Turkey's 14 per cent. Azerbaijan mainly exports petroleum products to Russia; see *Nezavisimaya gazeta*, 6 May 1998.
[47] An attempt was made to blow up a bridge in the new railway section in January 1998.
[48] Renat Karchaa, 'Talking at Cross Purposes', *WarReport* 52, p. 17.

pan-Caucasian meeting of governors, republican leaders and parliamentary delegations of the North and South Caucasus and southern Russia *krais* took place in April 1998 in Djohar. North Caucasian leaders hope to commit Chechnya to controlling crime, Chechen leaders are trying to persuade the participants to lobby Moscow to fulfil its financial commitments to Chechnya, while South Caucasian leaders (only Georgia and Azerbaijan have taken part so far) seek yet another alternative to Moscow. In the words of Shamil Basayev, 'even if we do not make any decisions here, the fact that we got together and talk to each other is good'.[49]

In the North Caucasus the Union of the Chambers of Commerce and Industry of Southern Russia, Adygeia, Dagestan and North Ossetia was created in January 1998.[50] The leaders of Kabardino-Balkaria, Karachaevo-Cherkessia and Adygeia signed an agreement in July 1997 to create an Inter-parliamentary Union to boost economic and cultural cooperation and to counterbalance the Chechen–Dagestani alliance.[51] The populations of the three republics are closely related to one another and contain sizeable Russian communities. North Caucasian leaders have initiated cooperation with other southern Russian regions; for instance, Valeriy Kokov of Kabardino-Balkaria signed a treaty with Astrakhan *oblast* in April 1998.[52]

Chechnya is a driving force in initiating new relationships with the South Caucasus. Motivating factors include transport routes, the common interest in counterbalancing Russia's influence and the exploitation of trade and energy opportunities. The Chechen leadership started to deal directly with the Azerbaijan authorities in October 1997. Chechen Deputy Premier Vakha Arsanov met with Azeri officials in Baku in order to discuss assistance in restoring the Chechen oil, power-generating and machine-building sectors. The visit was followed by two trips by President Maskhadov to Baku in November and March. Relations between Djohar and Tbilisi have also intensified. This is aggravated, however, by the Chechen support of Abkhazia in the Georgian–Abkhaz conflict, which makes the Georgian authorities distrustful of Chechnya's long-term loyalty, although Chechen Vice-President Vakha Arsanov apologized for participation in the war in Abkhazia and accepted Georgian territorial integrity. Chechnya is also interested in exporting its oil through an alternative link, which does not cross Russian territory. To this end it proposed building a Djohar–Tbilisi pipeline, which would join up with the Baku–Supsa pipeline. Mountainous terrain, the likely costs and turmoil in South Ossetia make such an option very problematic, however.[53]

[49] Briefing on the meeting of Caucasian leaders in Djohar, Ministry for Nationalities of Dagestan, April 1998.
[50] *Nezavisimaya gazeta*, 23 January 1998.
[51] Igor Rotar, 'Ochag spokoistviya v zone nestabil'nosti', *Nezavisimaya gazeta*, 13 May 1998.
[52] The treaty even envisages Kabardino-Balkaria's access to the Caspian Sea and the stationing of its vessels in Astrakhan.
[53] Shirvani Basayev discussed these ideas again during his visit to Baku in April 1998; see *Nezavisimaya gazeta*, 22 April 1998.

There is also a range of Muslim alignments. Various Islamic integration projects were launched in 1997 by rival Chechen politicians. Islamic Nation, headed by Movladi Udugov, is presented as an organization of all the Muslims of the Caucasus. Other projects openly proclaim *jihad*, among them the Caucasian Confederation created by Zelimkhan Yandarbiyev and Salman Raduyev's Caucasian Home.

To sum up:

- The economic assets of the North Caucasus are few, and the resource base is narrow. This limits prospects for sustainable economic development.
- Federal subsidies may soon cease because of Russia's diminishing capabilities and also because they do not bring the intended economic and political results.
- Infrastructure is crucial for the region's development, but the policies adopted by individual republics increase competition and create new obstacles in the communication system. The prospects for regional cooperation are bleak.
- Economic security, especially that of the pipeline network, is fragile. The deteriorating security situation in Dagestan may make the Russian government abandon the oil pipeline bypass plan.

Social problems

Social indicators in the North Caucasus are among the lowest in the Russian Federation. The most important social problems are unemployment, income polarization and migration.

Unemployment

The region has an oversupply of labour, and birth rates in the mountains remain high.[54] The population is very young: in Dagestan 32 per cent are below 15, while the 15–25 age group makes up 18.5 per cent of the population.[55] In Soviet times some of the excess labour force was employed in the defence industry, while others used to travel around the USSR as casual labourers or traders. Most have had to return, further swelling the workforce. Dagestan has 30 per cent unemployment (up from 26.7 per cent in 1997)[56] and the republic's trade unions estimate that 56 per cent of young people are unemployed. Dagestan has the second highest and North Ossetia the third highest unemployment rate in the Russian Federation. The situation is

[54] Birth rates in Ingushetia are 13.9 per 1,000 while the Russian average is -5.6 per annum, *Regiony Rossii* (Moscow: Situatsionny tsentr pri Presidente RF, FAPSI, 1997).
[55] The infant mortality rate is 19 per 1,000 live births.
[56] M-S. Gusayev, interview in *Nezavisimaya gazeta*, 12 May 1998. In 1996 the rate was 24 per cent, while the Russian average was 9.3 per cent.

similar in the other republics. The most extreme case is Chechnya. According to Ivan Rybkin, Chechnya 'is emerging with difficulty from a condition of war: 100 per cent of its youth are unemployed, as are 80 per cent of the male populace as a whole, and they possess 90,000 guns.'[57]

Poverty and income polarization

Statistically, the North Caucasian republics are the poorest in the Russian Federation (in Dagestan per capita income was 31 per cent of the Russian average in 1996). There are, however, many rich people with modern cars and luxurious houses.[58] The picture is one of acute social polarization and a widening gap between rich and poor leading to an increase in social tension. Those relying on their salaries in the state sector have a hard time, since salaries have not kept pace with inflation and are often in arrears.

The tabulation below shows households' purchasing power rates according to region in 1997 out of a total of 88 regions.[59]

Tumen Region	1st
Adygeia	70th
Karachaevo-Cherkessia	79th
Kabardino-Balkaria	81st
Ingushetia	82nd
North Ossetia	85th
Dagestan	86th

What rational strategies can the population employ in the face of increasing social pressures? Some people write petitions to the State Duma, vote for Communists who are seen as standing for social justice or go on strike in places where industry still works (there were 285 strikes in Dagestan in 1996). Others turn to religious radicalism: not only Islam but also various Protestant sects are growing in popularity.[60]

Migration

Many impoverished villagers opt for immigration to the towns in the hope of securing better job opportunities. Internal migration from rural into urban areas and from the highlands to the lowlands has been on going for the last 20 years, but the Soviet system used to regulate migration flows.

[57] Rybkin speaking on the Itogi news programme, February 1998, cited by John Dunlop in 'The Uncertain State of Russia–Chechen Relations', *Analysis of Current Events* 10: 3–4, March/April 1998, p. 17.

[58] For a colourful view see Valerii Tishkov, 'Taking Responsibility', *WarReport* 58, 1998, p. 71.

[59] The two last places are occupied by two autonomous districts in Northern Buryatia. The source for this is *Izvestiya*, 7 March 1998.

[60] See Svetlana Akkiéva, 'Kabardino-Balkaria: religioznye problemy'.

Immigration into the North Caucasus grew from 1989 (when there was anti-Caucasian violence in Central Asia) and reached its peak in 1995 when a massive displacement occurred within the region as a result of fighting in Chechnya.[61] From 1996 emigration overtook immigration and at present the migration balance is negative. Those who are leaving are the local intelligentsia and the Russians, a rapidly shrinking minority.[62]

In the nationalist conflicts among the indigenous groups, concessions to accommodate new demands were made at the expense of the local Russians. There is no official pressure on Russians to leave; in fact, measures are taken to encourage them to stay. In reality, however, all the important economic and socially prestigious positions, as well as viable political appointments, are being monopolized by indigenous groups. Only token Russians remain in formal positions, while the real power lies firmly with representatives of the titular groups. Moreover, many Russians used to work in the numerous defence enterprises in the region. They were left unemployed in changing economic circumstances when heavy industries collapsed and economic activities started to concentrate mainly around the trade and service sectors. Their ability to adapt to the new situation has also been hampered by the absence of extended family networks and lack of free capital. Moreover, Russians more readily consider emigration as few have roots in the North Caucasian republics and some have places to go back to in the rest of Russia.

The Russian community in Chechnya is a special case. According to various estimates, between 30,000 to 50,000 still live in the republic, mostly in Naurskii and Shelkovskii *raions*. They are subject to widespread abuse, pressure to give up their houses, robbery and murder, while the Chechen law enforcement structures are unable to offer effective protection. The Russian community has petitioned the federal authorities to organize an urgent evacuation of Chechnya and for resettlement assistance, but their appeals have fallen on deaf ears.[63] It is hypocritically assumed that Chechnya is a part of the Russian Federation and therefore Russians cannot face any specific problems. The government ruling is that only those who have proof that they left between 12 December 1994 and 23 November 1996 (i.e. during the actual fighting) are eligible for the necessary status and compensation payments. According to Federal Migration Service estimates, 60,000 families left Chechnya for good as a result of the war, but only 14,000 are eligible to receive compensation.

[61] Dagestan received 153,600 DPs in 1995.

[62] Timothy Heleniak, 'Internal Migration in Russia during the Economic Transition', *Post-Soviet Geography & Economics* 38: 2, 1997, and Robert Kaiser, 'The Nationality Composition of Migration in Russia's Republics', paper given at ASN Annual Convention, New York, April 1998. Yeltsin also admitted that Russians are leaving the North Caucasus almost as quickly as they are leaving the former USSR republics; see *Monitor* 4: 109, 8 June 1998.

[63] Natalia Airapetova, 'Kreml' ravnodushno vzirayet na sud'bu russkogo naseleniya Chechni', *Nezavisimaya gazeta*, 22 April 1998.

Prospects for development

In mid-1999 the prospects for sustainable development look bleak. The slow pace of the development of energy resources in the Caspian Sea basin (it may take another ten to fifteen years for wealth to be generated) and the relatively limited stake of the North Caucasus in Caspian energy transportation mean that major early revenue flows are unlikely to emerge from that source. The main hurdles in energy transportation are the effects of the volatile internal politics of the region. While the uncertainty over the future route prevails, the regional actors are likely to use the pipeline question to achieve their own political goals. The oil and gas resources of the North Caucasian region itself are small compared with the Caspian Sea basin's overall reserves, and political instability, a hostile investment climate and lack of infrastructure will make it very hard to attract investment. The best hope of the oil producers in the region may be to sell oil and gas locally in southern Russia when the industrial demand there increases, but that is not likely to be soon.

Social and economic conditions have increased political tensions, while the regional leaderships' strategy has been to lobby Moscow for subsidies to have the problems solved rather than to employ self-sufficient survival strategies. The republics' governments lack control over local administrations to stimulate or implement local initiatives. For Moscow the reasons for subsidizing this borderland region are unlikely to change in the near future, but its capacity to deliver is rapidly diminishing given the general economic situation in the country. Moreover, many of the social tensions are not a product of the Russian federal policy but are indigenous to the region and will stay so irrespective of Russia.

5 RUSSIA'S DILEMMA OVER THE NORTH CAUCASUS

Since 1991, Moscow policy-makers have been searching for solutions to the problems of governance in the North Caucasus. At present, the region is seen as more of a liability than an asset for Russia, but its geopolitical and geo-economic significance is too high for Moscow to relinquish control over the area. Moscow's current political objectives in the North Caucasus are the preservation of Russia's territorial integrity, preventing the situation in Chechnya from destabilizing regions outside its boundaries, containing crime and protecting communications (especially pipelines) and access to the Caspian Sea. The federal authority's dilemma is how best to maintain these interests while taking account of the likely effects for the political development of the Russian Federation as a whole of the possible strategies for the North Caucasus. Since 1991 the federal government's policies have undergone different stages: management of ethnic relations, attempts to regain control of the region by force, and budget federalism. Moscow's present perception of the region is that it is a gangster stronghold where crime feeds into ethnic tensions, and a bastion of radical and increasingly militant Islam.

Asymmetric federalism

Policy options in a multi-ethnic state

All the Soviet successor states have been faced with a choice between civic and ethnic concepts of the state. There has been also a clear tendency to break away from the pattern of Soviet nationalities policy, the constitutional provisions of which were marked by a fusion of ethnicity with political authority. While the Soviet system did not officially recognize ethnicity as a significant affiliation that affected social opportunities, it supported cultural identities and also used ethnicity for political purposes. The political establishment of new Russia tried to put relations between its various peoples on a new footing.

Russia faces a choice between three main policy options in dealing with the issue of ethnic diversity; these options will be referred to as modernization, pluralism and centralism.[1] Russia can adopt what might be described as a modernization strategy,

---

[1] This argument was developed by Clem McCartney in Anna Matveeva and Clem McCartney, *The Lezgins: A Situation Assessment Report* (London: International Alert, 1997), but it has a wider significance than the Lezgin issue.

which treats ethnic diversity as a historical feature which should not have any place in a modern state. According to this strategy, decisions should be made on the basis of equity and fairness across the whole community, and the state should protect the rights of all citizens as equal individuals in society, with advancement in society and in the institutions of government made on the basis of merit. From this perspective, ethnic identity should not be the basis for either decision-making or the allocation of rights and privileges. In fact, strategies recognizing ethnic differences would be positively harmful since they would endorse distinctions between sections of society and give expression to divisive tensions. This would be particularly problematic, if not dangerous, during the stage of state-building when efforts are being made to develop a common identity and loyalty to the new state. It is argued that policies based on the modernization strategy would not encourage social or political mobilization on the basis of ethnic identity. Yet these policies do not rule out recognizing the role of culture as a stabilizing force in society which helps the individual to have a sense of belonging to his or her community.

The pluralist argument maintains that divisions exist in society and that they need to be recognized and catered for in order to prevent confrontation from developing between the different sections of the community. In situations of scarcity actual or perceived inequalities might develop in regard to the opportunities available to the community. Existing identity markers such as ethnicity and language provide a readily available basis for explaining discrepancies between individuals' social, political and economic circumstances, thereby leading to a sense of inter-community rivalry and a mutual sense of resentment even when there is no objective basis for such assumptions. Thus policy-makers should recognize ethnic or other such identity differences as a significant factor and consequently make differential provisions on the basis of those categories to compensate for actual or potential inequality. In some cases, this may include the exercise of autonomy by a group over its internal affairs or a federal form of state structure.

The third approach is similar to the modernist one in that traditional identities are seen as dangerous. Thus according to the centralist strategy, control should be exercised from the centre in order to ensure that the whole community supports the state. This tends to result in a more authoritarian system in which opposition of any kind is suppressed either by force or by social pressure. From this perspective, the way to deal with ethnic identity is to deny its existence. In such a situation, if ethnic differences are deep-seated, they may be resistant to efforts to suppress them and become a focus for opposition.

The policy dilemma is that in trying to avoid divisive tendencies in the state, each approach may in fact encourage ethnic tensions and conflict. Acknowledging ethnic diversity may provide a justification for ethnic demands, which in turn may intensify them. Yet ignoring or suppressing ethnic diversity may stimulate feelings of resentment or grievance, which can escalate into demands for ethnic rights.

The Russian central government broadly adheres to a pluralist perspective, as reflected by its constitution and political practices, although this approach produced certain centrifugal effects and resulted in what Richard Sakwa calls the 'republican-ization' of Russia. The constitutional outcome of this perspective was asymmetric federalism.

Patterns of centre–periphery relations

The Russian Federation is far more mono-ethnic than the USSR: 83 per cent of the population is ethnic Russian. The federal structure based on ethno-territorial federalism was inherited from the Soviet era. When the Russian regions became important players on the political scene, the structure came under increasing strain, as tension and competition arose among the territorial regions and the ethnic republics.

Since the period of perestroika, the North Caucasian ethnic republics have sought to elevate their status and several have proclaimed sovereignty. In a drive to preserve the territorial integrity of the Russian Federation, in spring 1992 Moscow introduced a Federation Treaty which consisted of three sets of agreements reflecting the unequal distribution of power between the various levels of subjects of the Federation. The ethnic republics received the greatest degree of autonomy, which caused resentment among the territorial regions. In response, the constitution adopted in December 1993 aimed to reduce the disproportionate shift of rights to the republics. As a result of this step the republics lost the sovereign title, but retained most of their rights – for example to presidency, parliament, constitution, language policy and state symbols.[2] Despite the legal provisions, relations continued to be characterized by a struggle for power, and the regions *de facto* acquired similar powers to those enjoyed by the ethnic republics. The strongest leaders of the republics and regions managed to sign special power-sharing treaties with Moscow. In the North Caucasus both Kabardino-Balkaria and North Ossetia managed this in 1994 and 1995 respectively.[3] The legal outcome of the power struggle was that among all the ethnic republics only Tuva has a constitution that does not contradict the federal constitution.[4] The State Duma deputies have discussed whether Russians ethnic republics should also be created.[5]

[2] For a description of this earlier period of the formation of centre–periphery relations see Neil Melvin, 'Russian Federation' in the *World Directory of Minorities,* Minority Rights Group, 1997, pp. 294–312.
[3] There were 46 power-sharing treaties in 1998. In 1994–5 they were signed only with the republics, but in January 1996 Kaliningrad and Sverdlovsk broke the ground for the regions.
[4] About half of the 16,000 pieces of legislature contradict the federal law.
[5] Vladimir Zorin, the chairman of the Duma Nationalities Committee, appealed to MPs not to contrast the regions with the republics, but the deputies retaliated with an attempt to look into who gets direct transfers and why; see Petr Pliev, 'Russkim v Rossii – status respubliki', *Nezavisimaya gazeta,* 20 February 1998.

A precise division of powers remains more an aspiration than a reality. Subjects of the Federation have from 30 to 100 federal agencies on their territory which are a dual responsibility, the most important being the Ministry of Interior, Federal Security Service (FSB), tax police, anti-monopoly committee, postal services and transport, all to a varying extent controlled by the centre.[6]

The regional elites were further strengthened in 1996 when directly elected regional leaders became members of the Federation Council. It seemed that they had a corporate interest struggle against the centre for more rights and privileges. However, the regional elites failed to unite on this basis and were prevented from mobilization by latent conflicts within them. Instead, vertical and horizontal groupings among the regional elites competing for power and money have emerged. The enhanced role of the presidents within their republics, and their concentration on their own narrow interests, did not facilitate integration processes either but made it easy for the centre to split the regional elites.[7]

Nevertheless, the republican elites were the principal winners. As neither law nor political conventions determine a clear division of powers between the centre and periphery, in the republics the centre can be blamed for every negative development because it did not clearly delegate power and specify its responsibilities.

Asymmetric federalism was exercised through a number of agencies which emerged in Russia in the early 1990s. The Ministry for Regional and Nationalities Policy was the official body charged with policy-making for the regions. Its significance varied according to the political weight of its head. The authorities originally believed that threats would be posed by the kind of inter-ethnic conflicts which had contributed to the demise of the USSR, so the emphasis of the ministry was to deal more with various nationalities issues (for instance, with ethnic Russians outside Russia) and less with policy towards the regions.

The institution of presidential representatives was intended to provide the president with 'eyes and ears' throughout the Federation. It was introduced in 1991, but the initiative met with strong opposition from the republican authorities in the North Caucasus and failed to materialize.[8] It was revitalized during the 1996–7 elections for governor, which meant that the governors were no longer directly accountable to the centre and fell out of the line of authority. In 1997 it expanded to cover a greater number of regions, and a special department in the presidential administration was created to coordinate the representatives' activities. In July 1997 a new regulation

---

[6] Dagestan has 17 federal agencies – this is a typical situation.

[7] 'Problema sub'ektnosti rossiiskoi politiki', *Reforma* Foundation Report, *Nezavisimaya gazeta*, 19 February 1998, p. 8.

[8] In 1993–6 the institution practically withered away, as presidential representatives were used as a bargaining chip in the deals struck by the centre with the regional authorities. For more on the subject see Nikolai Petrov, 'Namestniki – predstaviteli presidenta', *Politicheskii Landshaft Rossii* 2–3, Moscow Carnegie Center, September–October 1997, pp. 17–23.

defining the role and functions of the presidential representatives was adopted. This stated that they were responsible for 'coordination of the activities of republican and federal bodies, reinforced control over the implementation of the federal budget, control over the use of the federal property, and they are to play an increased role in the appointment of personnel to the federal bodies in the republics'.[9]

In December 1996 Petr Marchenko, a former governor of Stavropol *krai*, was appointed presidential representative to Adygeia, Dagestan, Kabardino-Balkaria, Karachaevo-Cherkessia and Stavropol *krai*. Marchenko is also a member of the Military Council and is permanently based in Stavropol, relying on support and information from his advisers in the ethnic republics. Many advisers are former KGB officers from these republics and as a rule are deeply involved in local interests. In North Ossetia and Ingushetia the office of the representative developed out of the Interim Administration, which was itself a structure of the Russian federal government. It deals exclusively with the resolution of the Ossete–Ingush conflict.[10] The objective of counterbalancing the power of republican and regional chief executives by reinforcing the system of presidential representatives has not achieved the desired results. The extensive rights and privileges of the presidential representatives have not translated into real power, which firmly lies with the republican presidents *vis-à-vis* the federal centre.

Since the end of the war in Chechnya the federal body vested with overall responsibility for dealing with the republic has been the Security Council (under its secretary Ivan Rybkin), often nicknamed 'the Ministry for Chechen Affairs'. At the same time Rybkin was a presidential representative in Chechnya, until the attempt to treat Chechnya as a 'normal' subject of the Federation was made and Valentin Vlasov was appointed instead. The Russian government also had a special representative for Chechnya, Georgii Kurin, dealing with economic matters. This complex arrangement was made more so by the creation of two separate commissions for Chechnya. Any functional distinction remained unclear and it is likely that the duplication reflected Yeltsin's pattern of vesting two different bodies with the same task in order to play one off against the other.

Factors affecting policy-making

There are a number of factors affecting federal policy-making towards the North Caucasus. These apply across the whole political spectrum, irrespective of the current stance of various actors and decision-making bodies.

---

[9] Other functions include informing the centre of local developments (for instance, listing those federal programmes which have not been implemented and passing them on to Moscow), control over the implementation of the federal laws and providing expertise on whether local legislature contradicts the federal one.

[10] The first representative was A. Kovalev, former governor of Voronezh region.

- *The region's status as a frontline military district.* There is a perception that major threats come from the south, specifically from the Caucasus, and in this sense the North Caucasus has emerged as Russia's most vulnerable borderland.[11] The defeat in Chechnya demonstrated that large troop concentrations do not necessarily provide security and that the military component of Russian power is seemingly broken beyond repair.[12] The perception of the southern flank, exposed and vulnerable in the face of external and internal destabilization, touches a sensitive chord in Russian military and political thinking. Anatolii Kvashnin, Chief of the General Staff, has described how 'the threats from the south are the most dangerous ones. Here economic, demographic, ethno-national and separatist factors are at work. We in the General Staff cannot fail to take this into account.'[13]

- *The effects of the military débâcle in Chechnya.* The aftermath of the war created a 'Chechen syndrome' – policies aimed at the prevention of a repetition of the military intervention scenario at all costs. The present attitude of the Russian elites and general public towards Chechen independence is one of indifference, but there is a moral consensus that the war was wrong.

- *The pipeline issue.* The Caspian pipelines are regarded in Russia as a highly charged political issue, a new round of the great game between East and West following NATO enlargement. There is a view among the political elites in Moscow that 'Caspian oil with all its economic significance is only a cover for the global political objective of the present day – the resurrection of Russia's power'.[14] The choice between the pipeline routes readily lends itself to a zero-sum perspective. In such a framework, the battle for the selection of the northern route turns into an issue of international prestige, and Dagestan and Chechnya assume an exaggerated strategic significance. Pipeline politics is portrayed as an arena for the activity of external forces, determined to undermine or damage Russia, and local tensions in the North Caucasus are believed to be fomented by these outside forces.

[11] Roy Allison, 'The Chechenia Conflict: Military and Security Policy Implications', in Roy Allison and Christoph Bluth, eds, *Security Dilemmas in Russia and Eurasia* (London: RIIA, 1998), pp. 241–80.
[12] Pavel Baev, 'Conflict Management in the Former Soviet South: The Dead-End of Russian Interventions', *European Security* 6: 4, winter 1997, p. 118.
[13] Interview with Anatolii Kvashnin, *Argumenty i Fakty* 23 June 1998.
[14] 'Kaspiiskii globalnyi pas'yans', Report of the Institute of the CIS Countries, *NG-Sodruzhestvo* 4, 1998, p. 4.

Resolution of the conflict with Chechnya

The crucial factor in the resolution of the conflict with Chechnya is that the war of 1994–6 was a straightforward conflict for political secession and did not lead to an outbreak of inter-communal violence. Russia is the only state in the CIS involved in a violent conflict where an anti-war movement has emerged.[15] The poorly conducted war caused anger among the general public, and the mass media, as well as prominent political and military figures, campaigned against it. Even the military did not feel a moral superiority over the enemy and were not sure whether justice was on their side. Chechnya is not regarded as a valuable piece of territory dear to the hearts of ordinary Russians (the Crimea was such a territory, yet Russians came to terms with its loss). The obstacles to allowing Chechen independence are political and constitutional rather than popular.

The flimsy moral grounds for intervention and the devastation inflicted on the republic led Moscow to adopt a more conciliatory stance in the aftermath of war. This also brought political moderates into key positions in negotiations with Chechnya, but even for them the territorial integrity principle is sacred. There is little appreciation on the Chechen side that the infringement of territorial integrity is a highly charged issue for any state and that states – and here the international community is in full sympathy with Russia – do not easily accept such symbolic losses. Sergei Blagovolin reflects the attitude of the political community in Moscow: 'There is no more definitive criterion of strength or weakness of a country than the ability to protect its own vital interests on its own territory.'[16]

At present one issue is whether a further undermining of Russia's territorial integrity can be justified to the federal political establishment, including the State Duma, the Council of Federation and foreign policy bodies, and what kind of effects this might have for a whole range of other territorial problems. Another issue is whether secession could spread. So far this has not been the case, but the appearance of separatists in Dagestan, however marginal, has seriously undermined the position of those who argued that Chechnya's separatist drive is a special case .[17]

For independence to be formally established, a number of practical issues have to be resolved.

- The border between Chechnya and Ingushetia has to be formally delimited. Some settlements in Chechnya might like to join the economically more prosperous Ingushetia (or vice versa).

---

[15] Active cooperation between Russian and Chechen NGOs has emerged, for instance between the Committees of Soldiers' Mothers and others.

[16] Sergei Blagovolin, 'Pryamaya i yavnaya ugroza Rossii', *Nezavisimaya gazeta*, 19 February 1998.

[17] Emil Pain, 'Etnicheskii separatism – osobyi vid konflikta mezhdu regionami i tsentrom', in J. Azrael, E. Pain and N. Zubarevitch, eds, *Evolyutsiya*, pp. 30–52.

- The question of the return of the Naurskii and Shelkovskii *raions* to Stavropol *krai* is likely to arise and will also have to be addressed. Given their own independence bid, it would be difficult for the Chechen leadership to appeal to the 'inviolability of the existing borders' principle.
- Border installations on Stavropol *krai* and Dagestani borders have to be built – something which will take time and money.

To all intents and purposes Chechnya is already an independent state and Russia shows no interest in controlling the territory or its people. It might be argued that nothing practical can be gained by international recognition. However, symbolic value is very significant. Chechens believe that they have won their right to independent statehood in arms and blood, that they are a nation and that real nations should have a recognized statehood and a seat at the UN.[18] They also believe that international law would protect them in the event of an attempt by a reassertive Russia to use force in future. NATO action in Yugoslavia, which sparked public debate over the possible partition and independence of Kosovo, has boosted hopes for Chechen independence.

No significant progress on the issue of political status has been made since the signing of the Treaty on Peace and the Principles of Mutual Relations between the Russian Federation and the Chechen Republic of Ichkeria in May 1997. The treaty is a no-use-of-force agreement but not a comprehensive peace settlement, although the Chechen side insists that the document recognizes Chechen independence. Moscow is in no hurry to resolve the status problem, nor does it aim to regain control over the rebellious republic. The heated Russian debate on policy options which centred around the issue of how to preserve territorial integrity by peaceful means (and how to save face) has lost its prominence and is presently concentrated on the spread of instability in the region. Yeltsin's decree, adopted in December 1998 and abolishing the previous decree of September 1997 for preparation of the Treaty on Devolution of Powers between Bodies of State Power of the Russian Federation and the Chechen Republic, acknowledged the reality. The current ruling suggests that Moscow has stopped pretending that Chechnya is a normal subject of the Federation and openly admits that the republic is interested in nothing but outright independence. It also accepts that previous presidential and governmental commissions for Chechnya proved futile.

Meanwhile, the absence of a tangible Russian threat has had a demoralizing effect on the Chechen leadership, which kept a united front during the war. At present Chechen senior political and military figures seem too engaged in internal feuds to be

[18] Edward Walker, *No Peace, No War in the Caucasus: Secessionist Conflicts in Chechnya, Abkhazia and Nagorno-Karabakh*, Strengthening Democratic Institutions Project, Harvard University, JFK School of Government, Cambridge, MA, February 1998, p. 48.

able to put an issue on the political agenda in Moscow. Their attempts to achieve foreign recognition were a failure.[19] The immediate option is to make it awkward for Moscow to sustain its current claim that Chechnya is a part of the Russian Federation. In such circumstances, public executions decreed by *sharia* courts, the proclamation of the Islamic Republic, territorial claims on Dagestan, the spillover of crime through 'administrative borders', Maskhadov's international visits and the public demonstration that Russian federal laws are not applicable on the Chechen territory all help to distance Moscow from the breakaway republic.

The issue of killings and hostage-taking, however, dominates Russian–Chechen relations, as well as the external relations of the breakaway republic. The Russian–Chechen dialogue was suspended after Valentin Vlasov, presidential representative in Chechnya, was kidnapped in May 1998. The kidnapping and murder of Akmal Saidov, a staff member of the Russian delegation to Chechnya, in September 1998, made the federal politicians even less willing to talk. Negotiations resumed on Primakov's initiative at his meeting with Aslan Maskhadov in Vladikavkaz in October. Vlasov's release, which followed in November, was symbolic. On the one hand, it demonstrated that Russian power structures deal directly with criminal groups in Chechnya, bypassing the Chechen legal authorities, which expressed their surprise. On the other hand, it revealed power struggles in Moscow by unveiling the Ministry of the Interior's attempt to counterbalance the influence of the media tycoon and ex-CIS executive secretary Boris Berezovskii in the North Caucasus and seize the initiative from him in releasing hostages held in Chechnya.[20] Berezovskii's part seemed to be the most controversial one: he played a crucial mediating role in the freeing of many hostages, most notably the British aid workers John James and Camilla Carr, yet the Chechen authorities repeatedly accuse him of paying ransoms which lead to new kidnappings. More importantly, Berezovskii seems to operate in his private capacity as an independent actor, not taking orders from anybody, including the Russian government.

Another wave of crime negated the previous modest achievements. As noted above, four employees of Granger Telecom were beheaded by their abductors in December 1998 after an unsuccessful attempt by the Chechen authorities to free them. This series of killings and kidnappings, in the words of Aslan Maskhadov, has nullified the results of the Chechen war and all of his government's diplomatic work.[21] Any moral superiority which Chechnya gained during the war with Russia has been severely

[19] See Charles Blandy, *Chechen Status – Wide Differences Remain*, Conflict Studies Research Centre, P27, February 1998, pp. 35–7. Even the Baltic states, not reknowned for their Russian sympathies, abstained from recognition.

[20] BBC Monitoring Service, 22 November 1998, quoting 'How Boris Berezovskii fell out with counterintelligence. The scandal over the FSS has roots in the North Caucasus', *Segodnya*, 21 November 1998.

[21] *Monitor* 4: 227, 9 December 1998.

undermined. The kidnapping of Deputy Interior Minister Gennadii Shpigun in March 1999 halted negotiations with Moscow and led it to threaten to use force for the first time since the war ended.

Less spectacular, but no less controversial, is Russia's aid to the breakaway republic. The Chechen side claims that no economic aid has reached them, while Valentina Matvienko, Russian vice-premier responsible for the social sphere, has stated that targeted finance had been allocated and sent to Chechnya, but no financial report was ever sent back. Meanwhile, Chechen financial investigators suspect that money has been stolen on both sides of the chain, and that this process started during the war. Their activities are severely constrained by pressures from both the Russian and the Chechen sides, as each suspects them of siding with the other, and probably both have something they would like to conceal.[22] There are also signs that at least part of the Chechen establishment has started to move more closely into Russia's orbit. Alongside other autonomous republics the Chechen government, starved for cash and facing a hard winter, sent a representative to a meeting in Nalchik for the first time in December 1998, to discuss urgent social needs in the North Caucasus.[23] If Moscow abstains from using coercive methods against Chechnya and internal turmoil in the republics continues, a willingness to return to the Federation might gradually emerge among segments of its population.

Current policies

Since the end of the Russian–Chechen war the federal policy, having gone through the stages of management of ethnic relations and then the use of force, has viewed the North Caucasus from both a security and an economic perspective. Under Sergei Kiriyenko's government the objective was to revive the Federation through budgetary federalism and the streamlining of centre–periphery relations. Financial considerations started to prevail over purely political ones even under Chubais in Chernomyrdin's government. Thus the abolition of a free economic zone in Ingushetia in July 1997, which had been created to gain the loyalty of the Ingush leadership in the conflict with Chechnya, was welcomed by the federal tax offices as well as the tax offices of the neighbouring *krais* of southern Russia. Another intended tool was the emphasis on the federal programmes controlled by the centre and the reduction of direct transfers into republican budgets. However, as soon as any danger of destabilization appeared, the financial allocations were resumed.[24] The focus of the federal political

[22] Abdulhamid Khatuev, 'Gde i kak ischezayut den'gi dlya Groznogo', *Nezavisimaya gazeta*, 11 December 1998.

[23] *Nezavisimaya gazeta*, 10 December 1998.

[24] Sergei Stepashin, responsible for managing the situation in Dagestan, met with the Dagestani Muslim clergy, including Nadirshakh Khachilayev, in the aftermath of the violence to assure them that the money for direct transfers to the republican budget was on its way; see *Nezavisimaya gazeta*, 2 June 1998, p. 2.

elites has now shifted from a fear of secession to a determination to eradicate crime in the North Caucasus. This trend, which started during Kiriyenko's government (March–August 1998), continued under Primakov's administration.

Fight against crime

Moscow's new resolve meant that the Ministry of the Interior gained prominence, and in June 1998 President Yeltsin gave its head, Sergei Stepashin, overarching responsibility for the North Caucasus. After a period of relative inactivity (due to the political crisis in Moscow and the formation of a new government), a number of developments unfolded in the autumn of 1998. In Dagestan a fight against crime was initiated by Vladimir Kolesnikov, Deputy Minister of the Interior, and was supported by Moscow's political establishment.[25] This campaign was also supported by the Dagestani leadership, who were eager to get rid of rivals for power in the republic but did not want be too involved in such a dirty business. The campaign started in September 1998 with the arrest of prominent members of Dagestani elite, both formal and informal, including the Khachilayev brothers. Over 30 arrests followed on charges of terrorism, abuse of office and embezzlement. The fight against crime in Dagestan had started to fade by the beginning of 1999, however, leaving the locals with the impression that the Dagestani authorities had hoped simply to remove their political competitors with Moscow's help. Behind-the-scene deals have since been struck between offenders and the Dagestani leadership and some suspects released in exchange for their help in freeing important Russian hostages in Chechnya. In other cases nominal sentences are expected. Vladimir Kolesnikov has lost most of his zeal and advised the public to hold the Dagestani authorities more accountable for the fact that criminals managed to occupy senior positions in the republic.[26] Sergei Stepashin, appointed head of the Russian government in May 1999, is likely to stress the 'law and order' component in relations with the North Caucasus.

Policy-making by the Primakov government

While *realpolitik* prevails behind the scenes, conceptual discourse dominates the public domain. Moscow seeks to promote regional cooperation among the North Caucasian authorities, which normally compete against one another for federal subsidies. In 1997 Moscow started to develop a concept of macro-regions and attempted to look at the North Caucasus as a whole rather than to deal with the republics individually.

[25] According to Kolesnikov, his brigade filed 80 criminal cases, arrested 67 people and freed 33 hostages; see *EWI Russian Regional Report* 4: 5, 11 February 1999.

[26] Kolesnikov at the press conference in Makhachkala, January 1999, cited by Enver Kisriev, 'Vladimir Kolesnikov vnov' priekhal v Dagestan', material submitted to the *Bulletin*, January 1999.

This is a challenging task given that politics in the republics has grown more disparate since Soviet times and presents a variety of very different challenges. Thinking at the federal level is unfocused and this lack of focus was reflected in a draft blueprint of the State Nationalities Policy of Russia in the North Caucasus, prepared in January 1998 by the Nationalities Ministry but later abandoned. The shelved blueprint was reactivated in autumn of 1998 and Yeltsin ordered its early adoption.[27] The Ministry itself survived a number of reorganizations during 1998. After the spring reshuffle of the government it was renamed the Ministry for Regional Policy and Nationalities Affairs in an attempt to streamline centre–periphery relations via a more coherent system of budgetary transfers. These efforts were abandoned after the August economic crisis. Splitting the Ministry into two parts in September 1998 – one dealing with territories (the Ministry of Regional Policy) and the other with ethnic relations (the Ministry of Nationalities), spelled the end of the policy of making federative relations more homogeneous and applying the same rules to everybody. The Nationalities Ministry, headed by Ramazan Adbullatipov, a Dagestani and an ex-vice-premier of the Russian government, was intended to deal with the North Caucasus, as well as the other ethnic republics. Adbullatipov, however, stated that Chechnya was not his ministry's responsibility, and that the Ministry of Regional Policy should be in charge of that particular issue.[28]

A similar turnover of people and policies has taken place in the department of presidential administration responsible for regions. Rapid changes in leadership have meant no one has been able to pursue a firm policy line or take any long-term view. The centre of decision-making moved from the presidency to the government as a result of the August crisis and Yeltsin's weakness, but shifted back following Yeltsin's recovery and Primakov's sacking. At the same time, the government's attention has been distracted by major economic problems. For centre–periphery relations the agenda is dominated by such issues as securing tax from richer regions, balancing the ambitions of the governors in the emerging presidential race and controlling potential unrest in strategically important areas like large cities. None of these factors apply to the North Caucasus and the region is likely to remain a low priority for the government in the near future.

Some token activities continue nevertheless. In December 1998 a Commission for Social and Economic Development of the North Caucasus was set up by a decree issued by Boris Yeltsin. The commission was headed by the then First Vice-Premier Vadim Gustov, who was responsible for the regions, and included Ramazan Abdullatipov and Vyacheslav Mikhailov, First Deputy Head of the Security Council and ex-Nationalities Minister, as his deputies. The commission, another body in a chain of

[27] Interfax, 6 November 1998.
[28] Interfax, 25 September 1998.

similar projects, was created to stabilize the social situation and address the development needs of the region, as well as to coordinate the activities of various federal agencies engaged in the North Caucasus.

In contrast to the federal establishment, Aleksandr Lebed, governor of Krasnoyarsk *krai* and a likely presidential contender, shows considerable enthusiasm for the region. He has created a Peace-Making Mission for the North Caucasus and called for a series of steps to be implemented, such as organizing a Ministry for North Caucasus Affairs.[29]

Resolution of Ossete–Ingush conflict

After years of stalemate, decisive attempts at resolution have been made by the republican leaderships. This has led to mixed results: more political will towards settlement was generated, but the security situation deteriorated sharply in June–September 1998. This coincided with the economic and political crisis in Moscow. The capital's reaction to violence in North Ossetia was to dispatch Sergei Stepashin to the region to mediate between the two sides. The head of the Russian Federal Migration Service, Tatyana Regent, undertook a mission to organize aid provisions for the victims of violence and also initiated a survey among Ingush DPs to determine whether people were prepared to wait indefinitely to return or might be willing to be resettled elsewhere in Russia. The survey, well-intended as a policy planning measure, provoked a hostile reaction from the Ingush, who interpreted it as a reflection of Moscow's decision to preserve the existing situation and to give up any ideas of repatriation. They also assumed, not without reason, that the rise of anti-Caucasian sentiment could make the social atmosphere in Russia unfavourable for resettlement.[30]

In 1998 Evgenii Primakov took personal control of developments in the North Caucasus. He called a meeting in September in Moscow, which was attended by Russian power ministers and the presidents of Ingushetia and North Ossetia. Ruslan Aushev proposed a status of condominium for Prigorodny, i.e. joint control of the area, but this was rejected by the other participants.[31] Further shuttle diplomacy, such as Primakov's visit to Vladikavkaz in October and the January 1999 Security Council meeting involving the republican presidents, finally led to the signing in Magas in March 1999 of an agreement on the repatriation of all Ingush DPs to their places of original residence by December 1999.[32]

[29] *Krasnaya zvezda*, 15 January 1999, cited in BBC Monitoring Service, 17 January 1999.
[30] Abu Gadaborshev, 'Lishnie rty', *Nezavisimaya gazeta*, 3 December 1998.
[31] Interfax, 21 September 1998.
[32] *EWI Russian Regional Report* 4: 8, 4 March 1999.

Whither Russia?

Russia's diminishing capacity to influence political, economic and social developments in the North Caucasus is increasingly apparent. It lacks both political leverage and the coercive power to manage an increasingly volatile situation. Moreover, internal feuds in the region and lack of progress towards regional cooperation make Moscow politicians weary of further engagement: they would prefer North Caucasian politicians to deal with their own troubles. Ramazan Adbullatipov bitterly complained that 'there are no fraternal relations' in the North Caucasus. He also advised the North Caucasian republics to rely on their own resources, in effect suggesting that federal assistance could be significantly reduced.[34] This would have grave implications for the republics, which are at present heavily subsidized by Moscow, and endanger the republican leaderships who are dependent on their capacity to reallocate federal subsidies.[34]

Meanwhile the resurgence of militant Islam in the North Caucasus, in sharp distinction to other Muslim parts of Russia, has developed into a major problem. The radicalization of Islam was unleashed by the war in Chechnya and spread over the borders of the breakaway republic where it found fertile ground among the disaffected and desperate citizens of the North Caucasus. For any government, even one less chaotic than Moscow, Islamic radicals present a formidable challenge. Islam is a growing concern for Moscow, and events in Dagestan, as detailed in Chapter 3 (see p. 37), have caused considerable alarm. At the same time, federal politicians are ambivalent on the best course of action to take, nor do they have many means at their disposal. So far, Moscow has preferred to let the republican authorities manage the problem.

Military issues

Military withdrawal is, perhaps, the most striking current trend. After the collapse of the USSR, many regiments once based in Eastern Europe were relocated to the North Caucasus and the region turned into a frontline military district with a high concentration of troops. The war in Chechnya reinforced militarization even further. At present Ministry of Defence troops are located around the perimeter of Chechnya and include the 58th Combined Arms Army (based in Vladikavkaz), the 136th Motor Rifle Brigade (based in Buinaksk) and the 205th Detached Motor Rifle Brigade (based in Budennovsk). Meanwhile the 101st Brigade and the 247th Airborne Regiment (MoD) have withdrawn from Chechnya to Stavropol *krai*.

---

[33] Abdullatipov, at a press conference on the North Caucasus in October 1998, quoted by *Nezavisimaya gazeta*, 24 October 1998.

[34] Dagestan received less than half the money due in June, and almost nothing in July, according to Eduard Urazayev, spokesman for Dagestani government; see *Nezavisimaya gazeta*, 4 September 1998.

In 1998, however, the situation started to change. A deciding factor was the increasing threat to the security of Russian troops. In Dagestan the 136th Brigade has come under fire several times since December 1997, when Dagestani Islamic militants claimed responsibility. The group of Interior Ministry Troops drawn from various Russian regions has also been attacked a number of times.[35] In April 1998 a regiment of strategic bombers (MoD) was withdrawn from Mozdok to Saratov and as a result the airfield in Mozdok lost its status as the aerial gateway to the North Caucasus.[36] In Stavropol *krai*, which is already highly militarized as a result of the redeployment of over 50 units over the last five years, a permanent operational group is being set up using troops from various power ministries. The group, numbering 10,000, is under the overall command of the Interior Ministry. It covers, among other sectors, border areas in Stavropol *krai* adjoining Chechnya and Dagestan.[37] Three rapid response divisions of the Interior Ministry are stationed in southern Russia's part of the North Caucasian military district (which includes Stavropol and Krasnodar *krais*, Rostov region and the ethnic republics of the North Caucasus) in Novocherkassk, Krasnodar and Pyatigorsk. The armed forces seem to have decided that Stavropol *krai* should be turned into a military stronghold to which troops pulled out of the North Caucasus can be reallocated and which, in the end, might become a defensible frontier for Russia.

Borders

The crucial question is where Russia's border lies at the moment. An answer is necessary to determine which agency is supposed to guard which section. Most troublesome is the administrative border with Chechnya. The Dagestani leadership is in the process of finding an adequate response to the Chechen challenges, such as spillover of instability and calls for integration. In October 1997 the administrative regime on the border between Chechnya and Dagestan was tightened and since then the border has been closed temporarily on a number of occasions. Another measure, adopted in November 1997, was to dig a trench along the low-lying sector of the border. The trench is designed to construct a physical barrier against the looting of cattle and the hijacking of cars, but it is just a first step in the creation of border installations. The Dagestani Deputy Interior Minister Magomed Omarov complained that effective border protection is complicated by the absence of a legal

---

[35] *Monitor* 4: 222, 2 December 1998.
[36] ITAR-TASS, 10 April 1998.
[37] BBC Monitoring Service, interview with Russian Deputy Interior Minister Stanislav Kavun, 30 October 1998, quoting *Ekho Moskvy*, 28 October 1998. When asked whether a formal border would be established, he responded that in this case a political decision would have to be made and that it all depended on what policy Moscow pursued towards Chechnya.

74

foundation for enforcing it: the border is *de facto* an international frontier, but has the status of an administrative one and can be protected only by local police forces and Interior Ministry troops.[38] The border guard troops have no direct role in defending the border and appear in no hurry to take on such a burden.[39] The sections of the border separating Chechnya from Dagestan, North Ossetia and Ingushetia are guarded by a temporary joint grouping of Russian forces in the North Caucasus, and only the 114 km section between Chechnya and Stavropol *krai* is protected by Interior Ministry troops.[40]

The situation on the Russian–Georgian border is marked by disputes over contraband spirits. The 'alcohol war' reached its climax in August 1998,[41] but subsided following the economic crisis in Russia. At the same time, an agreement on the withdrawal of Russian border troops from the Georgian–Turkish border was signed in 1998, and the formal transfer of installations and border demarcation is going ahead. Russia's decision in October 1998 to move the border post in Lower Zaramag closer to the Georgian border was implemented without incident.[42] All Russia's marine border forces of the North Caucasus military directorate have been withdrawn from Georgia and the ground troops withdrawn are to be reallocated to the North Caucasus Military District.[43]

The delimitation of the border with Azerbaijan is under way but will take years to finalize as some communications run through Azerbaijani territory. The Russian delegation on border negotiations with Baku includes representatives from Dagestan and the Foreign Ministry consults the Dagestani authorities on any controversial issues. The establishment of the 5km 'alienation zone' has been postponed because of protests by the local population, but the decision is still in force. Only 70 per cent of the border is delimited at present, and local disputes between farmers and border guards over land cultivation arise every so often.[44] Other issues include the distribution of water resources from the Samur river as well as cross-border trade. Despite the

---

[38] Ekaterina Tesemnikova and Vladimir Torin, 'Buinaksk zhivet v osade', *Nezavisimaya gazeta*, 5 February 1998.

[39] Fully operational posts are only located in one section where the borders of Georgia, Chechnya and Ingushetia all meet. Steps taken by other agencies include military police units based in Stavropol *krai*, helicopters reconnaissance flights every day and armoured columns on the roads. However, as Aleksandr Chernogorov, governor of the *krai*, reflected bitterly, 'I envy those regions that have posts, border checkpoints, normal conditions etc.' Interview on NTV, 19 April 1998, cited by BBC Monitoring Service, 20 April 1998.

[40] Russia TV Channel, Moscow, 8 May 1998, cited by BBC Monitoring Service, 9 May 1998.

[41] Dmitrii Nikolayev, 'Velikaya spirtovaya voina', *Nezavisimaya gazeta*, 20 August 1998.

[42] Interfax, 4 November 1998.

[43] ITAR-TASS, 15 October 1998.

[44] In December 1998 over a hundred people attempted to cross the border near the Garakh village to attend to lands the Dagestanis consider to be theirs; see *Nezavisimaya gazeta*, 4 December 1998.

recent opening of an additional customs post in Tagirkent, commercial traffic congestion remains a problem. An interstate agreement regulating these two issues is being prepared.[45]

Impact on individual republics

Although the general trend is that of withdrawal, it will affect different republics to differing degrees. With regard to North Ossetia, it is safe to conclude that Moscow's policy will tend to favour the republic. Evgenii Primakov and Aleksandr Dzasokhov have enjoyed a good relationship since the latter served as a Soviet ambassador to Syria in the late 1980s – an area of special interest to Primakov, who also served as a people's deputy to the Supreme Soviet from North Ossetia. Primakov's decision to meet with Aslan Maskhadov in Vladikavkaz instead of Nazran suggested that Russia wished to reconfirm that North Ossetia is its favoured spot in the region.[46] In contrast, the significance of Ingushetia as a means of reaching the Chechen leadership has diminished following turmoil in Chechnya and the lack of any sense of urgency in Moscow political circles to negotiate its status. Although Ingushetia's free economic zone status has been abolished by Moscow, its economic dissociation from the centre has already taken place. President Aushev was determined to conduct a referendum in February 1999 for the nomination of local police chiefs and to legalize local customs that are considered criminal offences under federal law.[47] This prompted Yeltsin to issue a decree prohibiting the referendum. Ingushetia has demonstrated considerable independence in its legal provisions *vis-à-vis* the federal centre: its constitution gives its president the right to direct foreign policy and introduce a state of emergency, as well as declaring that republican laws take precedence over federal ones.[48] Aushev is trying to initiate a judicial conflict with Moscow which would legalize local legal practices and enable the republic to slip out from Russia's judicial control.

Dagestan is the region where, given its own present weakness, Moscow might have concluded that the cost of maintaining stability is too high.[49] According to *Komsomol'skaya pravda*, 'Russian power structures are evacuating everything of value from the republic'.[50] About 500 Airborne Troops are currently stationed in the republic, but their commander, Colonel General Georgii Shpak, favours their

[45] Milrad Fatullaev, 'Gosgranitsa – tozhe rynok', *Nezavisimaya gazeta,* 4 December 1998.
[46] *IEWS Russian Regional Report* 3: 44, 5 November 1998.
[47] Such customs include bride abduction and carrying a dagger; see 'Is Moscow Losing Patience with Aushev?', *RFE/FL Caucasus Report* 2: 7, 16 February 1999.
[48] *IEWS Russian Regional Report* 3: 47, 24 November 1998.
[49] There is a view that the Russian pull-out from Dagestan can be explained by Moscow's doubts about the loyalty of units stationed in the republic; see *Red Alert, Global Intelligence Update,* 27 October 1998.
[50] *Komsomol'skaya pravda,* 21 October 1998.

withdrawal.[51] No decisive attempts have been made to control the Dagestani–Chechen border; instead Moscow prefers to allocate funds to the Dagestani authorities to recruit local Interior Ministry forces. The arming of the local population and *de facto* creation of self-defence units by national movements and local authorities have not produced a firm reaction from the government in Moscow.

The appointment of Sergei Stepashin as prime minister in May 1999 was greeted with caution in the North Caucasus, where local leaders and the population at large preferred Primakov. Stepashin was the main initiator of the Russian military intervention in Chechnya, making it awkward for Aslam Maskhadov to continue a political dialogue and leaving him vulnerable to accusations of collaboration by the Chechen opposition. Moreover, Stepashin's 'efficiency record' in the region is rather poor since none of his efforts to enhance security there have led to any tangible result.

Conclusion

If the region is in flux, Moscow's policies are in flux as well – it is grappling with forces which are beyond its control. As a result its reactions have been varied and often contradictory. This is partly explained by the relatively low priority given to the North Caucasus within the country, and by institutional and personal confusion in decision-making. However, developments in the region are difficult for the federal centre to comprehend and make it hard to develop a coherent approach, while Russia's current economic situation constrains the means to implement policy, even if more cohesion emerges at the top.

In the 1990s the notion of the territorial integrity of the Russian Federation has been put to the test, first by the war in Chechnya and second by political disorder in the region. By the end of the decade, the situation in Dagestan has become a major challenge for Russia. Whether its withdrawal from Dagestan is tactical or strategic will depend on Russia's ability to pull itself out of the current political and economic crisis and restructure power relationships. The vacuum in Dagestan is unlikely to be filled by the Western powers, and the continuation of internal Chechnya-style feuds is the most likely scenario. If turmoil continues for a number of years and no effective authority is established, Dagestanis might welcome a revitalized Russian influence. However, a new Russia might in the end decide that it is easier to rule within its more natural, ethnically more homogeneous borders and maintain Dagestan as a satellite rather than a fully-fledged constituent part of the Federation.[52]

[51] *Novye Izvestiya*, 23 September 1998.
[52] Such a debate is already under way; see, for instance, Anatolii Petrov, 'Pobeditelnoye otstupleniye', *Kommersant-vlast'*, 11 August 1998, pp. 9–12.

The Caspian pipeline seems to have lost its strategic role. There is a growing understanding that pipelines are relatively unimportant in the context of much larger security challenges. Politicians in Moscow are more inclined to wait and see how events unfold than to venture into new interventions. The business community feels that it does not have to control internal developments in the territories to be able to receive revenue from oil and gas transit and that mutually beneficial cooperation is possible even in an extremely difficult political situation.

6 CONCLUSION

In the North Caucasus the political situation during the 1990s enabled the republican elites to exploit the opportunities presented by the Soviet collapse. It also unleashed forces in the region which were beyond the control of the authorities. Conflicting national projects, elite rivalry and new means to secure access to power made the situation increasingly volatile. Throughout the decade, Moscow has been struggling to come to terms with these processes, and its search for adequate policies has made it adopt varied responses at different times and with varied applications. This was a clear departure from the Soviet *modus operandi*, pursued primarily by political means. In the Soviet era, Moscow created the local leaders and subjected them to strict control as well as giving them a stake in the centrally designed order. It also had enough leverage and awareness of ethnic interests to be able to manipulate them successfully. With the downfall of the communist system the new Russia lost the political means to influence developments. It had to rely on coercive power, which was in disarray, and on economic incentives, which were scarce. Moscow's capacity to address challenges has greatly diminished. This led to threats to the territorial integrity of the Russian Federation, as well as to developing centre–periphery relations. Economic security, especially concerning the viability of the energy supply routes and of transport infrastructure in general, was undermined.

As a result of developments in the last ten years, the political and social organization of the proto-states of the North Caucasus has become increasingly diverse and processes in them have been localized. Fragmentation, rather than integration, is the prevailing trend. Political order in the proto-states is extremely fragile, with one 'failed state' (Chechnya) already and Dagestan apparently heading in the same direction. The direct effects of Chechnya's *de facto* independence on other republics are relatively small, but its impact as a warning of what might happen if authority collapses is more serious. Internal stability in the near term will be affected by the ability of the leaderships to improve the economic and social situation and foster more inclusive politics. If the current decline continues, crime and destabilization may become rampant, and with it further political fragmentation and the collapse of government authority. The fragile stability will be put to the test when the present generation of Soviet *nomenklatura*, which is still in power in the North Caucasus, depart from the political scene and a new generation of politicians take over the top positions. Tensions within the region between various republics and *krais* are also likely to increase and competition rather than cooperation is the present mood. Prospects for regional stability and development depend on whether forces of change can be incorporated into some form of political order, or whether the existing pressures and strains lead to chaos.

The republics of the North Caucasus also acquired different political and social arrangements from the rest of the Russian Federation, be it introduction of the *sharia* justice system in Chechnya or legitimizing bride kidnapping in Ingushetia. The North Caucasus as a region has grown more inward-looking. Consequently, its people and politics have become more remote and more alien for the federal government. The ethnic Russians' exodus reinforces the process of distancing and creates disincentives for Moscow to enhance its commitment to the region. Local Russians prefer to leave and establish themselves elsewhere rather than fight for their position, and Russian policy follows this trend. At the same time, the criminal situation is deteriorating further and Islam is playing an increasingly conspicuous role. As the region emerges as a stronghold of Muslim radicalism within the CIS it not only challenges the Russian central government, but could also produce tensions among Muslims living in other parts of the Russian Federation.

The price Russia is prepared to pay for maintaining the North Caucasus is becoming an increasingly important issue. Soviet policy-makers would not even have considered such a question. The Soviet policy establishment demonstrated a remarkable determination to achieve its objectives at all costs, spending as much human and material resources as required. The present Russian authorities, in contrast, have to allocate resources to strategic priorities. The multiplicity of actors at the federal centre, and their institutional and personal interests, prevent concentration of effort and make it hard to identify priorities. The *de facto* loss of Chechnya influenced the perception of the North Caucasus as relatively unimportant for Russia's viability as a federation. Policy-makers in Moscow feel that Russia pays dearly for stability in the region and that the political and financial costs of maintaining the North Caucasus may be a burden the centre can no longer carry.

Russia is distancing itself from the Caucasus by default. Powerless to avert the region's fragmentation and the failure of its proto-states, Moscow's strategic retreat from the Caucasus is motivated by fear and is a reaction to further unwelcome developments, most notably the spillover of crime into the rest of the Federation and the Islamic challenge. It remains unclear what mechanism of disengagement can be devised. Radical options such as recognizing Chechen independence would require Moscow voluntarily to relinquish its territorial integrity. Moreover, apart from Chechnya none of the republics are pursuing separatist demands. There is virtually no anti-Russian nationalism at a popular level, as ordinary people have more grievances against their republican and local authorities, and still look to Moscow with a residual hope. The issue for Russia is how to disentangle itself from the region, while also saving face and remaining in control of the process of disengagement rather than being driven by events. The most likely outcome is a partial disengagement, whereby Russia retains only *de jure* authority over the North Caucasus without assuming responsibility for its internal developments, while all important facilities, including power structures, are withdrawn into the neighbouring *krais*, which in turn become Russia's *de facto* new borderland.

APPENDIX – THE REPUBLICS: A PROFILE

Adygeia

Capital	Maikop
Population	541.000 (1995)[1]
Adyge	22%
Russians	68%
Rural population	42%
Population density	59.3 persons per sq. m
Unemployment	2.4%
Population below poverty line	55.3% (8th lowest ranking in the Federation)
Income ratio of richest and poorest	12.8:1
Population annual growth	–3.9 per 1000 (1997)[2]

Adygeia, extending from the foothills of the Caucasus Mountains to the Kuban Plain, lies in the middle of Krasnodar *krai*, one of Russia's richest regions. Adygeia was continuously enlarged during the Soviet period and by 1989 was three times bigger than when it was founded in 1922 as an autonomous *okrug*.[3] In 1989 a group of Adyge intelligentsia founded the movement *Adyge Khas'e* which provided the basis for calls for the creation of the Adygei republic. Adyge Khas'e is a national movement of all Adyge (Circassian) peoples and represents the interests of the Adyge, Cherkess and Kabardins. Adygeia was upgraded to republican status in July 1991 and renamed the Republic of Adygeia in March 1992. Ironically, it acquired greater rights under the Federal Treaty than the *krai* within whose territory it lies. The republic

[1] Population figures for all the republics are taken from *Robertson's Russia & Eurasia Facts & Figures Annual*, volume 22, 1997, pp. 20–23; all other figures come from *Regiony Rossii*, Moscow: Situatsionny tsentr pri Presidente RF, FAPSI, 1997. The unemployment statistics, according to local observers, are well below the actual levels.

[2] Where 1997 data of population growth are cited, the source is Goskomstat of RF, in *Severnyi Kavkaz* 15, April 1998.

[3] Rieks Smeets, 'Circassia', *Central Asian Survey* 14: 1, March 1995, p. 119.

contains the highest concentration of Russians in the North Caucasian ethnic republics. Some Russians identified themselves as Kuban Cossacks and joined a wider Cossack movement, but enjoy little support among the majority of Russians in the republic.

The drive to separate from Krasnodar *krai* was motivated largely by the desire to elevate Adygeia's status *vis-à-vis* the federal centre and the opportunity to do so by playing the ethnic card. Recently the tensions with the Krasnodar *krai* authorities have been focused on the issue of Shapsug autonomy. The Shapsug, another Circassian people, had their own Shapsug *raion* within Krasnodar *krai* in 1924–45, but it lost its special status and was renamed Lazarevskii. The Adygeia republican authorities support their ethnic kin in their drive to revive the ethnic status of the *raion*, which the Krasnodar authorities do not regard as viable. However, relations between the top elite levels are friendly.

The Adyge, as the titular nationality, occupy strong positions in the power structures. Special privileges for the Adyge are guaranteed by the constitution adopted in March 1995. The representatives of the Russian majority competed successfully in the elections to the Russian Federation State Duma, but their capacity to contest power within the republic is limited. All presidential contenders were Adyge; this was facilitated by the constitutional provision that only a person who is fluent in both Russian and Adyge can run for presidency. The State Assembly, or Khas'e, consists of 45 deputies, 27 of whom are elected in single mandate constituencies (the remaining 18 are elected in dual-mandate constituencies). The Adyge's privileges are reflected in the way the constituencies are defined to ensure parity between Russians and the less numerous Adyge. The attempt to introduce a simple territorial definition of a constituency in December 1991 was met with fierce resistance by Adyge organizations. In the early 1990s Adyge national movements called for 50 per cent representation in the local legislature in order to guarantee rights for the titular nationality and to prevent assimilation, but this failed to become a constitutional provision.

The republican elite is still struggling to come to terms with unexpected sovereignty. The post-Soviet period has been marked by the gradual acquisition of property and office by those of the titular nationality and by the passage of a language law.[4] Adyge Khas'e is now is a loyal supporter of the existing order, and its whole outlook is directed towards cooperating with the authorities rather than challenging power. The Russian Union of Slavs of Adygeia was created in 1991 as a counterbalance to Adyge Khas'e, but failed to gain much political prominence.

Recent tensions are increasingly concentrated along social, not ethnic lines. The main political rivalry is unfolding between the existing power establishment and a strong local branch of the Communist Party of the Russian Federation which enjoys the majority in the State Assembly and also has two deputies in the federal State Duma.

---

[4] Mary McAuley, *Russia's Politics of Uncertainty* (Cambridge: Cambridge University Press, 1997), p. 114.

Karachaevo-Cherkessia

Capital	Cherkessk
Population	436,000 (1995)
Karachai	38%, 67% of them rural
Russians	37%
Cherkess	10%, 62% of them rural
Abaza	7%
Nogai	3%
Rural population	59%
Population density	30.9 persons per sq. km
Unemployment	3.8%
Population below poverty line	57.7%
Income ratio of richest and poorest	11.4:1
Population annual growth	1.0 per 1000 (1997)

The Republic of Karachaevo-Cherkessia is among the most ethnically diverse, and in the early 1990s had the highest number of sovereign republics proclaimed on its territory. The Karachai are traditionally highlanders, while other groups live in the foothills.[5]

Karachaevo-Cherkessia was the last subject of the Federation to elect a head of the executive. Formerly an autonomous *oblast* within Stavropol *krai*, it was granted republic status in July 1991. Moscow's original intention was to recreate separate Karachai and Cherkess autonomous districts as they existed before the deportation of Karachai in 1943, but the republican authorities managed to persuade Moscow that this would lead to a breakdown of inter-ethnic accord. After the Soviet break-up radical national movements called for further partition, such as the creation of a Karachai republic which was unofficially proclaimed in October 1991. In retaliation the Batalpashinskaya and Urupsko-Zelenchukskaya republics were proclaimed by the Cossack movements, while the Congress of Cherkess people declared a Cherkess republic and the Abazin Congress an Abazin one. The main winner of this parade of independence was the chief executive of the republic, the battle-hardened communist Vladimir Khubiev (a Karachai nicknamed 'the ever-lasting Caucasian president' who has ruled the republic for the last 19 years).[6] He succeeded in persuading Yeltsin that

[5] Most of Karachaevo-Cherkessia is made up of high mountains and it used to be a fashionable mountain ski resort in Soviet times. At present the republic is better known throughout Russia for the *Merkurii* enterprise, producing vodka and mineral water.
[6] 'Vechnyi President Kavkaza', *Segodnya*, 12 March 1998.

elections in the republic would cause major disturbances and the best option was to appoint the head of the republic (Khubiev) by presidential decree – a temporary measure that became a lasting feature. In a March 1992 referendum the effort to split the republic was rejected by 78.6 per cent of voters, although 75 per cent of the Russian populated Zelenchuk and Urup *raions* voted to leave the new republic and join Krasnodar *krai*.[7]

Throughout the 1990s the political history of the republic was turbulent but the battles were contained within the legal framework and never escalated into violence. In 1992 the Supreme Soviet, elected in the Soviet period as an *oblsoviet* (local council), failed to reconcile the viewpoints of the national movements on future electoral rules and instead decided to continue without elections. An attempt in 1994 to adopt a Law on the People's Assembly (the parliament) and develop electoral legislature failed after intense political battles between the executive, headed by Khubiev, and the Supreme Soviet, which represented the interests of various ethnic groups in the republic. Khubiev's attempt to introduce a popularly elected presidency in 1994 also failed. The discussions of the draft of the new constitution exacerbated legal disputes to a point of complete deadlock. Meanwhile, in December 1994 the Cherkess National Congress proclaimed the Cherkess Autonomous Republic within Stavropol *krai*, a move supported by the Russians and Abazin. Elections were suspended until 1995 because of the fear of upsetting inter-ethnic stability.

The federal authorities interfered in February 1995 and created a Conciliation Commission headed by Sergei Filatov, the Head of the Presidential Administration. The Commission prompted a new Law on Organs of Power in the Republic of Karachaevo-Cherkessia, according to which the single-chamber People's Assembly was elected in June 1995, consisting of 28 Karachai, 26 Russians, six Cherkess, six Abazin and three Nogais. An arrangement was worked out whereby the three branches of power would be headed by the representatives of the three main nationalities and the head of the republic would be appointed by President Yeltsin for a four-year term and approved by the People's Assembly until elections in April 1999. According to this law Khubiev was appointed in April 1995. The law was in direct contradiction to federal legislation, which envisaged the election of all the heads of the executive not later than 1996. The republic's constitution, adopted in March 1996, also provides for the election of the head of the republic and stipulates that the constitution takes precedence over any previous provisions.

There was virtually no force in the republic to challenge the incumbent before Stanislav Derev, a Cherkess and head of *Merkurii*, was elected in October 1997 as the

---

[7] The local authorities in Malokarachai *raion* refused to take part in the referendum, and a state of emergency had to be introduced to ensure the vote.

new mayor of Cherkessk.[8] The presidential elections in January 1998 in North Ossetia and subsequent power transfer also produced a domino effect. Two arguments emerged in the republic. One was to 'let Khubiev rule till 1999' and ensure peace and stability (an idea supported by the Karachai who saw him as a guarantor of continued federal compensation to the families of the deported). The other, uniting the rest of the population, was to demand elections.[9] A group of deputies of the People's Assembly appealed to the republic's Supreme Court and the court ruled to conduct elections no later than 1 September 1998. The Supreme Court of the Russian Federation overturned the ruling. The opposition called a protest meeting in January 1998, the first in the republic's history, in which 3 per cent of the electorate took part, to appeal directly to President Yeltsin.[10] Elections took place in two rounds, in April and May 1999. Khubiev lost in the first round, while Derev, the front-runner in April, was running against Vladimir Semenov (a Karachai) who won the second round amid widespread electoral violations and a campaign of intimidation.

Inter-ethnic relations are constantly an issue in the republic. Two main tendencies are apparent: one is the drive against the Karachai as the dominant titular nationality, the other is the tension between the Karachai and Russians (the two most numerous groups) on the one hand and small nations such as the Cherkess, Abazin and Nogai on the other. The latter are campaigning for a system of reservations and quotas, while Russians and Karachai support ordinary open-candidate electoral arrangements.

[8] Ekaterina Tesemnikova, 'Miting nedovol'nykh rukovodstvom Karachaevo-Cherkessii', *Nezavisimaya gazeta*, 21 January 1998.

[9] For more detail see L. Khoperskaya, V. Kharchenko, 'Politicheskii krisis v Karachaevo-Cherkessii', in *Bulletin* 6: 17, February 1998, pp. 39–41.

[10] 60,000 supporters' signatures were collected to hold the elections before June 1998 (the whole electorate of the republic is 250,000 voters). Vladimir Abuzov, 'Konflikt v Karachaevo-Cherkessii obostryayetsya', *Nezavisimaya gazeta*, 24 February 1998.

Kabardino-Balkaria

Capital	Nalchik
Population	790,000
Kabardin	48%, 55% of them rural
Russians	32% (less than 30% at present, estimate)
Balkar	9%, 41% of them rural
Rural Population	43%
Population density	63.2 persons per sq. km
Unemployment	3.6%
Population below poverty line	46.3%
Income ratio of richest and poorest	11.8:1
Population annual growth	2.6 per 1000 (1997)

The Kabardino-Balkar autonomous *oblast* was created in 1922 and was raised to the status of an autonomous republic in 1936. After the deportation of the Balkar, the republic was renamed Kabardin and a considerable area to the south was joined to Georgia. The status quo was restored with the Balkars' return in 1957.[11]

The main rivalry lies between the deported Balkars (the highlanders) and Kabardins (the lowlanders) who remained in the republic. While Balkars[12] are concerned with the restoration of historical justice inspired by the Law on Repressed Peoples and federalization or partition of the republic, the primary claim of Kabardins is an increase of political rights (in Soviet times the Kabardins had to share political positions with the Balkar on a one-to-one basis, although they are more than four times as numerous). In November 1991 the Balkar held a referendum calling for the creation of a separate Balkar republic, and Kabardins retaliated with an attempt in January 1992 to declare their part of Kabardino-Balkaria autonomous. Tensions over the possible division of the republic grew during 1992[13] but major violence was averted.[14] The main winners were the republican authorities who consolidated their grip on power while the national movements were exhausted by the struggle. The main losers were the Russians, at whose expense concessions to the ethnic movements

[11] Kabardins are the most numerous Circassian group, although even in Kabardino-Balkaria they do not constitute an absolute majority, see Smeets, 'Circassia'.

[12] There are 80,000 Balkars in the republic and another 20,000 outside.

[13] There was even an attempt to divide Nal'chik, at that time a 70 per cent Russian-populated city, into Kabardin and Balkar parts, but the sides could not agree on border delimitation.

[14] On the Kabardin and Balkar national struggle see Svetlana Akkieva, 'Lozung natsional'nogo samo-opredeleniya i politicheskaya bor'ba v Kabardino-Balkarii, 1989–1996', in *Pravo narodov na samo-opredeleniye: ideya i voploshchyeniye*, Pravozatshitnyi Tsentr 'Memorial' (Moscow: Zvenya, 1997), pp. 130–38, as well as discussion on pp. 152–5.

were made. In November 1996 the Balkar National Congress proclaimed independence and appealed to President Yeltsin to introduce direct presidential rule until new elections are held. The matter was settled by the decisive actions of President Kokov and by promotion of the Congress leader General Sufian Beppayev to a senior governmental appointment to distribute federal compensation to the families of the deported Balkar. He quickly became a loyal supporter of the Kokov regime.

The republic is headed by a president, elected together with a vice-president for a five-year period. President Kokov concentrates most power in his own hands. All presidential contenders were ethnic Kabardins. The local parliament, a bi-cameral Legislative Assembly, is modelled on the Federal Assembly. It is elected for a four-year term, the deputies serve full-time, and it consists of the Council of the Republic, to which the deputies are elected in 36 single-mandate territorial constituencies, and the Council of Representatives, to which elections are held in tri-mandate constituencies, the borders of which coincide with the administrative divisions in the republic.[15] The last elections were held in December 1997 and out of 72 deputies 39 are Kabardins, 16 Russians, 14 Balkar and three others.

The republican authorities made every possible effort to maximize Balkar representation in parliament.[16] The *raion* borders were drawn in such a way as to ensure privileged treatment for the Balkar. The lower chamber has more substantive powers than the upper one. The parliament has a special committee on Inter-Ethnic Relations, consisting of five Kabardin, five Russians and five Balkar, to monitor the situation in the republic and supervise the allocation of appointments to ensure parity.[17] The heads of the *raion* administrations (predominantly the former *raikom* secretaries) are hand-picked by the president from among the deputies of the local council and then proposed to the council for approval.

The bilateral agreement over divisions of powers between the federal centre and the republic was signed on 1 July 1994, the first of its kind in the North Caucasus and the second in the Federation. The republic also acquired free economic zone status, at least on paper. A constitution was adopted by parliament in September 1997, and a previous two-term restriction on presidency was abolished. Given the uneasy inter-ethnic relations in the republic and its severe economic decline, President Kokov, who is also the Deputy Speaker of the Federation Council, always emphasizes his closeness to Moscow.[18]

[15] There are nine *raions* in the republic and Nalchik, the capital, has three administrative districts. Each of these 12 is represented by three deputies and there are thus 36 deputies in the upper chamber.
[16] For an analysis of parliamentary elections see Svetlana Akkieva 'Itogi vyborov v parlament KBR', material submitted to the *Bulletin*, 1997.
[17] The senior appointments are divided as follows: the president is a Kabardin, the prime minister is a Balkar, the vice-president (a largely nominal position) is a Russian. In the Council of Ministers out of 21 ministers ten are Kabardins, four are Balkar, and three are Russians (there are other minority groups as well).
[18] Svetlana Akkieva, 'Prinyatiye novoi Konstitutsii', in *Bulletin of Network of Ethnological Monitoring and Early Warning of Conflicts*; subsequently in *Bulletin*, 4: 15, October 1997, pp. 26–7.

North Ossetia

Capital	Vladikavkaz
Population	663,000, half of them in Vladikavkaz
Ossetian	56%
Russians	27% (1997, estimate)
Ingush	5% (6,000 live in the republic = 1%)
Rural population	30%
Population density	82.8 persons per sq. km
Unemployment	2.8%
Population below poverty line	38.1%
Ratio of incomes of richest and poorest	8.3:1
Annual population growth	−1.1 per 1000 (1997)

The Ossetes are the only Christian North Caucasian people. They are the most integrated into the Russian political system and historically this has enabled the republic to serve as a mediator between other North Caucasians and the federal centre. North Ossetia was included in the Russian Empire in 1774, and even prior to that relations were those of allies. Vladikavkaz,[19] the most prominent city in the North Caucasus, was the centre of Terskaya *oblast* from 1863 and the main Russian stronghold in the area. North Ossetia had strategic significance as the base for Russian troops and for control over communications. The Darial Pass, a passage connecting the North and South Caucasus, is located in the republic and the main overland roads over the Caucasus range to Georgia, the Georgian Military Highway and the Transcaucasus Highway, pass through North Ossetia, thus increasing the importance of its location. At present it is the centre of the North Caucasus Military District. It is also the most densely populated, urbanized and industrialized republic in the North Caucasus.

Ossetes are a divided people with one group (Kudakhtsy) living in South Ossetia (Georgia) and the majority living in North Ossetia (Russia). The latter are comprised of two ethnic sub-groups, Irontsy and Digortsy, each of them possessing their own dialect. North Ossetia was the first autonomous republic in the USSR to declare its sovereignty in 1990, but was the last (in 1994) to drop the term 'Soviet Socialist' from its title.[20] It was renamed 'North Ossetia-Alania' in 1994 with an aspiration to drop 'North Ossetia' at some stage, so that the remaining 'Alania' would include both the South and the North. The unresolved conflict with the Ingush and the aftermath of

---

[19] Renamed Ordzhinikidze under Stalin, after the Georgian communist.
[20] Former President Akhsarbek Galazov frequently identified himself as communist.

violence in South Ossetia which resulted in a flow of ethnic Ossete DPs dominated North Ossetian politics in the early days of sovereignty. Officially registered DPs constitute 7 per cent of the population.

Moscow regarded North Ossetia as a strategic ally in the North Caucasus and half-heartedly supported President Galazov in his time in office. Galazov used his chance to prove the republic's loyalty to Moscow when North Ossetia served as the main base for the federal troops during the war in Chechnya. A power-sharing agreement, the fourth of its kind, was signed in May 1995 three days before parliamentary elections in North Ossetia, in order to boost support for Galazov. North Ossetes continue to be 'well-positioned' in Moscow political circles: General Kim Tsagolov is a Deputy Minister for Nationalities, and Sergei Khetagurov is Deputy Minister for Emergencies.

The republican constitution adopted in November 1994 stipulated that North Ossetia is a presidential republic and that the president, elected for a period of four years, is the head of the executive. The legislature, which numbers 66 seats, is also elected for a four-year term. Political developments in North Ossetia can be regarded as a notable exception in the North Caucasus. Relations between the executive and the legislature have always been stable. Aleksandr Dzasokhov won the presidential elections with 76 per cent of the vote in January 1998. In the parliamentary elections held in April 1999 seven ethnic Russians, one Armenian and one Kumyk were elected out of 66 deputies; the local branch of the Communist Party won the most seats, while the rest of the deputies were represented by enterprise directors, businessmen and bankers.[21] North Ossetia demonstrates a robust growth of political parties; there are even three communist parties in the republic. Although the parties do not produce a decisive impact on politics, their presence in the public domain is very visible.

Since the beginning of his time in office Dzasokhov has shown energy and initiative, and general support for the government has been boosted. Communication between the government and parliament has also improved. Dzasokhov pays careful attention to public relations, appearing on TV in order to communicate directly with people and to explain new policy undertakings. Two policy priorities were declared soon after his inauguration: to combat crime and to revitalize the economy. It is also assumed by the locals that Dzasokhov is well positioned in Moscow to ensure the smooth flow of subsidies to the impoverished republic.

---

[21] *EWI Russian Regional Report*, vol. 4, no. 18, 12 May 1999.

Ingushetia

Capital	Magas, former capital Nazran
Population	303,500[22]
Ingush	95% (estimate), officially 74.5%
Russians	1% (estimate), officially 13.3%
Chechens	10% (officially)
Rural population	70%
Population density	15.7 persons per sq. km
Unemployment	32.4%
Income ratio of richest and poorest	n/a
Population annual growth	13.4 per 1000 (1997)

The Republic of Ingushetia, the second smallest republic of the Russian Federation, was created in June 1992 as a result of the secession of the Ingush from Checheno-Ingushetia where they constituted a minority of 12.9 per cent. The decision to break away followed the declaration of independence by the Chechens in 1991. Deported together with the Chechens in 1944, on their return they found some of their lands allocated to North Ossetia. Frictions between Chechens and Ingush developed in 1989 as the Ingush did not support the Chechen bid for independence. Furthermore, the Chechen national movement was directed at the fulfilment of Chechen national aspirations and paid little attention to the concerns of the Ingush for their historical lands.

The history of Ingushetia since separation from Chechnya has been dominated by its conflict with North Ossetia. Relations with its Chechen neighbour have been cordial, and the Ingush were the most loyal supporters of the Chechens during the Russian–Chechen war. At the same time, border delimitation remains an issue. When the agreement was signed between the Chechen side and Russian federal authorities in November 1992, a *de facto* border was established according to the line which separated the Chechen and Ingush autonomous *oblasts* before January 1934. In December 1992 the parliament of Chechnya made a controversial decision to establish a border, but in January 1993 the Councils of Elders from both sides agreed to suspend the issue indefinitely. In 1996 in the aftermath of the war in Chechnya the Russian government again ruled that the border should be demarcated. A commission

---

[22] The population statistics are flimsy: estimates are that 230,000 live in the republic. According to the Office of the Representative of the Russian President in the Zone of the North Ossete–Ingush Conflict, Ingushetia *de facto* achieved mono-ethnic status; only about 3,000 are not Ingush. Interview with Victor Soloviev, adviser to the Representative, April 1998.

headed by the Minister of Nationalities was established for this purpose but has yet to visit the republic and start working.

The partition left the Ingush without an urban centre, as all the cultural and educational facilities remained in Chechnya's capital Djohar (formerly Grozny). The former capital of Ingushetia, Nazran, was founded in 1967 and has a population of only 71,900. The new capital, Magas, was inaugurated in 1998. The formation of organizations of state power in the republic was prompted by the North Ossete–Ingush conflict. Ruslan Aushev, the current president, was appointed as the first head of the Interim Administration in the Zone of Conflict in November 1992 but resigned in December over a disagreement with federal policy. He was elected president in February 1993. The constitution was adopted in February 1994 and in March 1994 the People's Assembly (local parliament) was formed. These developments laid the legal foundation for the new republic. President Aushev has made remarkable progress in building up the republic from scratch. There is no rival to challenge his power within the republic, and the main presidential contenders in the 1998 elections – Issa Kostoev and Mukharbek Aushev – were Moscow politicians. In December 1997 Aushev issued a decree making the law enforcement and judicial agencies directly accountable to him, and attempted to legitimize the decree with a popular referendum to be held on the same day as the presidential elections. The federal Supreme Court ruled that the decree runs counter to federal law. It based its decision on the provision that law enforcement and the judiciary are the joint responsibility of the federal and regional authorities and Aushev had no power to call a referendum. In retaliation Aushev refused to sign a power-sharing agreement with Moscow, scheduled for signature in March 1998, despite the fact that Moscow offered concessions to end the dispute over the control of power structures in Ingushetia.[23] The new parliament, numbering 21 members, was elected in March 1999 and consists of 18 Ingush, one Russian (forced in by Aushev instead of an Ingush) and two Chechens.

It is now clear that the secession drive was successful and there seems no chance that Ingushetia would ever want to join any of its neighbours. Despite its size, Ingushetia positioned itself well in the Moscow establishment. Mukharbek Aushev, an Ingush, is a vice-president of Lukoil, the largest Russian oil company. Claiming the need to combat 32.4 per cent unemployment,[24] the highest in the Russian Federation, President Aushev in 1994 persuaded Moscow to create a free economic zone in the republic (subsequently abolished in 1997) and attracted federal loans, making the republic exempt from paying federal taxes.[25]

---

[23] *IEWS Russian Regional Report* 3:10, 12 March 1998.

[24] This is an officially registered figure; the real situation may be much worse. See *Previewing Russia's 1995 Parliamentary Elections* (Moscow: Carnegie Moscow Center, 1995), p. 137.

[25] This status was abolished in 1997 and replaced by a less privileged 'favourable economic regime' zone.

Chechnya[26]

In 1989 the Chechens,[27] the largest ethnic group in the North Caucasus, numbered 899,000. In 1922 the Chechens were granted their own autonomous *oblast* (AO), but in December 1934 it was merged with the Ingush AO. Prior to their deportation in 1944, Chechens lived primarily in the mountain areas of Chechnya; many were resettled on the plains on return. Before the war, 40 per cent of the republic's population lived in Grozny where Russians made up half of the inhabitants. The remaining Russians lived in Naurskii and Schelkovskii *raions* (previously part of Stavropol *krai*), an area also populated by Nogais and Dargins, and Kumyks live in Groznenskii *raion*. Tensions traditionally lay between the lowland and highland Chechens; the former were mostly represented in the Soviet elite, and the latter formed a base of support for the secessionist movement of President Dudayev.

Having been a part of Checheno–Ingushetia where Chechens were in the majority (57 per cent), the republic declared its sovereignty in November 1990 and independence from Russia in November 1991. The independence movement was led by the Chechen National Congress. Its most prominent member, former Air Force General Djohar Dudayev, became President of Chechnya in 1991 in elections whose legitimacy has been questioned.[28] Following the declaration of independence and violence between supporters and opponents of the Chechen National Congress, Russian federal troops were sent to restore control but, owing to Chechen resistance and the refusal of the Russian Supreme Soviet to sanction a state of emergency and the use of force, the troops were withdrawn. By June 1992 all Russian troops had left the republic, leaving behind a large stock of arms.

A constitution, adopted in March 1992, stipulated Chechen independence. Chechen and Russian became the state languages and the Latin script, adopted at the time of President Dudayev's rapprochement with Turkey, replaced Cyrillic.[29] Dudayev issued a decree in January 1994 to rename the republic the Chechen Republic of Ichkeria.

On 10 December 1994 the Russian federal powers undertook a military intervention in the republic which lasted until 31 August 1996 and became the largest war in the former Soviet Union. Present relations between Moscow and Djohar are regulated by the August 1996 Khasavyurt Accords which established the cessation of hostilities, and the Moscow May 1997 Peace Agreement.

---

[26] There are no new statistics available for Chechnya at the time of writing, and the Soviet figures do not seem to reflect the present situation. The pre-war situation was as follows: population 862,200; Chechens 67%, Russians 24%, Ingush 2.3%; rural population 63%; population density 67.8 persons per sq. km.

[27] For the background on the Chechens see Johanna Nichols, 'Who are the Chechens?', *Central Asian Survey* 14: 4, 1995, pp. 573–7.

[28] On the elections see McFaul and Petrov, *Politicheskii al'manakh*, p. 298.

[29] 'Chechens', *World Directory of Minorities* (London: Minority Rights Group, 1997), p. 302.

The postwar parliamentary and presidential elections took place in January 1997 and brought Aslan Maskhadov, Chief-of-Staff and Prime Minister in the Chechen coalition government since October 1996, into power for a five-year term with a 63.6 per cent majority.[30] The Islamic Republic of Ichkeria was proclaimed in 1998 and the *sharia* system of justice introduced. The Arabic script is to replace the official Latin one. New Chechen passports started to be issued in January 1998.[31]

President Maskhadov has tried to concentrate more power in his own hands to push through reform and establish authority. In October 1997 he unsuccessfully appealed to parliament to grant him special powers for two years, including the right to impose a state of emergency, suspend the legislature and fire cabinet ministers and civil servants.[32] Another attempt to strengthen the executive and pacify internal feuds was made by Maskhadov in October 1997 by bringing Shamil Basayev, a prominent field commander and the hero of the Budennovsk hostage-taking, back into government. Basayev became acting premier and was asked to form a new government in January 1998. He took over domestic matters and focused on eradicating crime and improving the economic situation, while Maskhadov directed overall policy and relations with Russia. Basayev proved less successful as a civilian head of government than as a battlefield hero, however, and left his job in July 1998. The situation gradually slid out of the control of the central government, and the republic descended into chaos. Various opposition groups emerged, consolidated around prominent field commanders such as Salman Raduyev and Khunkar-Pasha Israpilov. In August 1998 Basayev broke off all relations with the Maskhadov government and joined the opposition, which by that time had revived the Chechen National Congress. Several armed clashes between Maskhadov loyalists and oppositionists took place around the towns of Gudermes and Urus-Martan, strongholds of various rebellious commanders. In October 1998, Basayev, Raduyev and Israpilov asked the parliament and the *sharia* court to impeach Maskhadov for 'treason', by which they meant his pragmatic approach to relations with Moscow.

In February 1999 Maskhadov introduced Islamic law into the republic by presidential decree. He also stripped the parliament of its legislative powers and abolished the post of vice-president. Maskhadov ordered the drafting of a new constitution based on the Koran and created a *Shura* (State Council), as an advisory body which the opposition was invited to join. The opposition had created an alternative *Majlis Shura* (Supreme State Council), to which they elected themselves and in which they allocated a seat to Maskhadov, but on condition that he resigned as president, claiming that presidency is incompatible with *sharia* law. The parliament, once the

---

[30] *OMRI Newsline*, 3 February 1997.
[31] *Monitor* 4: 1, 5 January 1998.
[32] *RFE/RL Newsline* 1: 145, 23 October 1997.

base of support for Maskhadov, refused to recognize the presidential initiatives as legitimate and continued to function as before. This created a triarchy, although no one possesses ultimate political authority over the entire republic.

Dagestan

Capital	Makhachkala
Population	2,150,000
Avars	28%[33]
Dargins	16%
Kumyks	12.9%
Lezgins	12.2%
Russians	6%[34]
Laks	5%
Chechens	4.5%
Tabassarans	4.5%
Azerbaijanis	4.5%
Nogais	2%
Agul	1%
Rutul	1%
Rural population	58%
Population density	42.2 persons per sq. km
Unemployment	24.1% (1996)[35]
Population below poverty line	71.8% (2nd highest in the Russian Federation)[36]
Income ratio of richest and poorest	26:1
Population annual growth	12.1 per 1000 (1997)[37]

[33] In the 1930s various mountain Ando-Dido groups were registered as 'Avars' during the period of Danialov, an Avar who was the first secretary of the republic and is reputed to have tried to create a titular nationality for Dagestan. Controversy persists as to whether these groups have much ethnic and linguistic closeness to the Avars.

[34] Interview with Magomed Salikh Gusaev, in *Ochag nash Dagestan* 1, 1996.

[35] This figure is given by *Sotsial'no-ekonomicheskoye polozheniye Respubliki Dagestan*, Committee for State Statistics of the Republic of Dagestan, 1997.

[36] The Russian Federation average is 22%.

[37] The population growth has slowed down: in 1989 it was 21 births per 1,000.

Dagestan, the largest of the North Caucasian autonomous republics of the Russian Federation, is situated on the western coast of the Caspian Sea. It is the southernmost territory of the Russian Federation. Dagestan means 'land of mountains', a name suggested by its largely mountainous terrain which contrasts with its flat, depopulated steppes in the north. The republic's most distinct feature is its ethnic diversity: it includes a total of 34 ethnic groups of either Caucasian or Turkic origin. None of the ethnic groups constitutes a clear majority, or occupies a dominant position, although the main rivalry is between lowlanders and highlanders.

Dagestan's constitutional and political arrangements differ significantly from those of the federal level and reflect the peculiar ethnic and social composition of the republic. The republic was the last one to declare sovereignty (May 1991) and its political culture remains highly conservative.

Dagestan's constitution, adopted in July 1994 by the Constitutional Assembly, stipulates that 'Dagestan is a sovereign united democratic state within the Russian Federation' and demonstrates a clear commitment to preserve inter-ethnic peace. Dagestan is the only region of the Russian Federation where the head of the republic is not elected directly by a popular vote, but is selected indirectly, in a two-stage procedure. The supreme authority in the republic is vested in the State Council, which consists of representatives of the 14 major ethnic groups (defined as those which have a written language) and is elected by the Constitutional Assembly for a period of four years. The position of Chairman of the State Council can be occupied by a representative of a single ethnic group for a period of four years and then has to be given up in favour of another group. The Chairman of the State Council. Magomedali Magomedov (a Dargin), is to all intents and purposes the acting president of the republic. According to the constitution, the terms of office cannot be extended. This provision for a collective presidency was introduced after an attempt to establish a presidency soon after the break-up of the USSR. This was twice rejected in referenda, in 1992 and 1993, because of the fear that it would put one ethnic group in a dominant position. A referendum on the same question in March 1999 brought the same result. The prime minister is also a member of the State Council and therefore precluded from being of the same ethnic origin as the chairman. The prime minister is in charge of the government and deals with economic and social issues, while the chairman of the State Council oversees the activities of the security structures and external relations.

A Security Council was introduced in Dagestan in August 1996 to 'combat organized crime and promote national security'. Its powers and functions are mainly directed towards minimizing the impact of instability in Chechnya. The People's Assembly, consisting of 121 deputies elected in March 1999 for four years, functions as a representative and legislative body, and also oversees the budget allocations.

Commitment to the principle of a four-year period in power for representatives of each ethnic group proved to be half-hearted. The first major test of the system came in

1996 when it became clear that Magomedov would not surrender power as he was supposed to under the conditions of his terms of office, but intended to continue for a further two years. The People's Assembly led by Mukhu Aliev, an Avar, initially put up resistance but soon all non-Avar deputies were offered special deals by the executive branch. They then voted for the extension of the office of chairman owing to 'exceptional circumstances' and the Avar deputies had insufficient votes to continue the fight.

The scenario was repeated in 1998 when Magomedov's extended term was due to expire. This time Ramazan Adbullatipov, an ethnic Avar and a deputy speaker of the Federation Council, launched a new attempt to oust the incumbent. He proposed the establishment of a directly elected presidency in the republic, hoping to gain the post himself. He managed to persuade Moscow that the situation in Dagestan was getting out of control and a strong hand was needed to bring it to order. On the basis of this he was promoted to vice-premiership of the Russian government in order to give him more political clout and make the population believe that he could bring an increase in federal care for the republic. This did not come about, however, as Abdullatipov had lost touch with Dagestan's internal politics, and even the Avars spoke against him.[38] Magomedov was successful in pressing the deputies (while Aliev was abroad) into making a constitutional amendment to abolish the provision that the chair of the State Council should be changed in favour of another ethnic group.[39] Magomedov was voted in for a second term in July 1998. This in effect means the power balance is secure in favour of the Dargins, the second ethnic group. Said Amirov, a prominent Dargin, has been a deputy prime minister of the republic, and was elected to the lucrative position of mayor of Makhachkala, which made him *de facto* number two in the republic. The abolition of the ethnic rotation principle also favours Amirov, who might aspire to become the next chairman. The Dargin group can be challenged only by the more numerous Avars, and in order to remain in power the Dargins will have to secure the support of a few other groups to oppose the Avars effectively.

[38] Interview with Gaji Makhachev in Igor Rotar, 'V Dagestane nevozmozhno presidentskoye pravleniye', *Nesavisimaya gazeta*, 28 November 1997.
[39] The letter requesting the abolition of the provision was signed by 108 out of 121 deputies. M-S. Gusayev, interview in *Nezavisimaya gazeta*, 12 May 1998. In 1996 the rate was 24 per cent, while the Russian average was 9.3 per cent.